Women and Human Rights in India

Women and Human Rights in India

Rachna Kaushal

Kaveri Books
New Delhi - 110 002

Rachna Kaushal (1972-)

First Published in 2000
Second Impression 2024

ISBN: 978-81-7479-025-5

Published by
Kaveri Books
4832/24, Ansari Road, Darya Ganj
New Delhi-110002 (India)
Tel: 011-23288140, 47072321
E-mail : info@kaveribooks.com
E-mail : kaveribooks@gmail.com
web : www.kaveribooks.com

Typeset at : Delta Book World, New Delhi - 110 002

PRINTED IN INDIA

Acknowledgements

I am happy to acknowledge my indebtedness to all those who helped me in carrying out this research work. I gratefully acknowledge the academic help, co-operation and the encouragement which was overwhelmingly given to me by the teachers of the Department of Political Science, A.M.U., Aligarh. I am specially indebted to Prof. T.A. Nizami, Chairman Department of Political Science, Prof. M.A. Kishore, Prof. M. Subramaniam, Prof. Iqbal Khanam, Prof. B. Rahamatullah whose help and encouragement was always with me in accomplishing this research work.

I would be failing in my duty, if I do not recognize the kind blessings and affection of all my family members, which is always boosting up my morale and is instrumental in continuing my efforts for a new achievement.

My gratitudes also go to my friends who always cheered me up and in fact devoted their time in carrying out the essential work of typing and proof reading. I am thankful to all of them.

Rachana Kaushal

Contents

Preface

The concept of rights and duties are perhaps as old as the civilization. Whether entitled under specific provision or name, mankind has always enjoyed certain basic freedoms & rights. Though the extent and the proportion of these rights may vary from time to time, person to person, place to place depending upon the prevailing politico-religious and cultural situations. With the passage of time the nature of rights and freedoms has undergone metamorphism. Today, the idea of Human Rights has gained so much of momentum that it encompasses all kind of rights; civil, social, economic and political. Thus removing the centuries old divide between them. The concept of Human Rights is anthropocentric. Whatever adds to the welfare and dignity of human beings is an ingredient of Human Rights. It provides for a uniform code of rights aiming at sustaining good, dignified life to a human being, transgressing all kinds of boundaries - physical, territorial, religious, gender, colour or race.

Though almost all the countries of the world provide fundamental rights to their citizens to enable them to lead a good, dignified life, but despite such provisions, there is exploitation, discrimination and violation of basic Human Rights. The harsh realities of human life are such that it is the woman who is discriminated, exploited and denied such freedoms and privileges, available to their counterpart for living a respectful life. This situation of discrimination and denial of Human Rights to the women is more grave and pathetic in the case of developing countries - particularly in Afro-Asia.

This study is an attempt to analyse the Human Rights with respect to women in India. It focuses on the nature and kind of violations of basic rights and freedoms to which Indian woman is subjected to despite the constitutional provisions & guarantees.

The first chapter of the study presents an evolutionary history of Human Rights in brief. It also gives an account of national and international provisions which guarantee Human Rights. The focus of the chapter is on the provisions which focus on the rights of the women particularly in India.

The second chapter is an assessment of status of women particularly of Indian women. This chapter also analyses rights and freedoms to which the Indian women are Constitutionally entitled. At the same time it tries to trace out the Constitutional discrepancy paving way for various kinds of discrimination and exploitation of the Indian women.

The third chapter assesses the kind of crimes committed against Indian women in Indian society in the presence of various Constitutional Safeguards available to them. This chapter also analyses the discrepancies of the laws enacted in India to protect the women against the gender specific crimes. Laws referring to crimes have been taken-up for analyses.

The fourth chapter deals with various other kinds of exploitation other than the crimes. The issues covered under this chapter are largely the result of our socio-religious fabric paving way for degrading further the already pathetic state of Indian woman.

The last chapter which is the conclusion throws light on various factors responsible for the violation of Human Rights in case of Indian women and the possible remedies.

The study is based on the published sources. The overall perspective of the study is to analyse the Human Rights and the situation of women in India. The purpose of the work is basically to understand the dynamics of women's exploitation in India. Despite my efforts and the help of others, some discrepancies could not be easily avoided I, therefore, alone shoulder the responsibility for the deficiency of the argument.

1

An Introduction to Human Rights

The concept of rights and duties is perhaps as old as the civilization. Whether entitled under a specific provision or name, mankind has always enjoyed certain basic freedoms and rights. Though the extent and proportion of these rights may vary from time to time and person to person depending upon the prevailing socio-religious, cultural and political set-up which are chief determinants of man's freedom and rights.

The concept of Human Rights is rooted in the most ancient values and religions of our heritage. However, Human Rights have an evolutionary history of about 2000 years which begins from the promulgation of Cyrus the Great. Though it passed through various stages of development, Magna Carta of 1215, the first written document relating to the fundamental rights of citizens, is often considered as the beginning of the struggle for Human Rights in an organised manner. Magna Carta, infact, provided a protective shield to the rights and freedoms of the chosen few, not of the general masses. American Revolution 1776, the French Revolution 1786 and the Declaration of Rights of Man and the Citizen 1789 are mainly considered as the landmarks in the developmental history of Human Rights. The other developments which contributed for the evolution of Human Rights was the humanitarian laws of warfare. From time to time various attempts were made to limit the horrors of warfare and to humanise it. Modern developments in this regard are traced to the efforts of Henry Dunant who after witnessing the horrors of

Salferino Battle organised a Conference in 1863 regarding the sufferings of wounded which ultimately culminated into Geneva Convention of 1864, and subsequently various other conventions like Hague Convention 1899, Geneva Conventions of 1927 and 1949 which laid down the humanitarian rules of warfare.

The term Human Rights as such is not found in traditional religions. Neverthless, theology presents the basis for a Human Rights Theory steming, from a law higher than the state and whose source is the Supreme Being: the Almighty God. However the beginnings of the Universal Human Rights Law came about as a result of the First World War. The terror waged by the Nazi regime led to internationalization of Human Rights. The term "Human Rights"-itself had not been mentioned in the Covenant of the League of Nations. It first appeared in the set of proposals agreed to in 1944 by the United Kingdom, the United States, the Soviet Union and China at Dumbarton Oaks in Washington, D.C. and was subsequently incorporated into the UN Charter. The Charter speaks of "fundamental human rights", "the dignity and worth of the human person", "equal rights", "justice", "social progress", "fundamental freedoms", the "self-determination of peoples" and the right of people to "self-government". Respect for Human Rights and fundamental freedoms was not like abstract ideas for the framers of the Charter. The war crimes tribunals in Nuremberg and Tokyo were unmasking harrowing "crimes against humanity"-Human Rights violations of monstrous proportions, such as savage medical experimentation, mass enslavement and "extermination". Founders of the United Nations focused on the role Human Rights should play in the conduct of nations. They knew first-hand that the dignity and worth of individuals and the right of everyone to basic freedoms were vital to destabilizing dangerous political situations and strengthening the Allied victory over the forces of fascism and intolerance.

UN Commission of Human Rights was set up in 1948 under the chairmanship of Eleanor Roosevelt which took up as its first order of business the definition of basic rights and freedoms. The first pillar of twentieth-century human rights law was adopted by the General Assembly on 10th of December 1948. Intended as a "common standard of achievement for all people", the Universal Declaration of Human Rights spelt out basic, civil and political rights and fundamental, economic, social and cultural rights which human beings everywhere were entitled to enjoy. As a statement of goals and principles, the Universal Declaration was a giant step. Although a declaration does not have the binding force of a treaty, the Universal Declaration of Human Rights has acquired universal acceptability. Almost all the countries have cited the Declaration or included its provisions in their basic laws or constitutions, and many Human Rights covenants, conventions and treaties concluded since 1948 have restated its principles. Among the rights and freedoms found in the 30 Articles of the Universal Declaration of Human Rights are—[1]

* The right to life, liberty and security of person;
* Equality before the law;
* Freedom of movement and residence;
* Freedom from torture or cruel, inhuman or degrading treatment or punishment;
* The right to seek in other countries asylum from persecution;
* Freedom of thought, conscience and religion;
* The right to vote and participate in government;
* The right to education;
* The right to work and to form and join trade unions.
* The right to an adequate standard of living;
* The right to health protection;
* The right to participate fully in cultural life.

The Universal Declaration of Human Rights further paved the way for signing of other agreements. The broadest legally binding Human Rights agreements negotiated under UN auspices are the International Covenant on Civil and Political Rights[2] and the International Covenant on Economic, Social and Cultural Rights.[3] Both were adopted in 1966 and entered into force in 1976. They took the

Universal Declaration a step further by making provisions legally binding and opening the door of international monitoring of Human Rights practices. Along with the Universal Declaration, they comprise the International Bill of Rights: the conceptual framework to which other Human Rights instruments have been added. The Second Optional Protocol to the Covenant on Civil and Political Rights was adopted by the General Assembly in 1989. The Protocol seeks to do away with capital punishment and is opposed by some countries on grounds that, the death penalty is consistent with their laws and customs and serves as deterrent to crime.

Some 70 Human Rights treaties and declarations have been negotiated under the aegis of the United Nations. One of them is the Convention on the Elimination of All Forms of Discrimination against Women[4] which covers measures to be taken to eliminate discrimination against women in political and public life, education, employment, health, marriage and family, and to embody the principle of equality in national legislation. Other than this various regional agreements have been signed which supplement and expand upon the international instruments, among them the European Convention on Human Rights and Fundamental Freedoms 1953; the Helsinki Accords, 1975; the American Convention on Human Rights 1978 and the African Charter on Human and People's Rights 1986. This march of mankind in the direction of Human Rights is still on. The issues of women who are being discriminated since ages are universally being emphasised. The fourth World Conference on Women organised in Beijing in 1995 highlighted the Human Rights abuses of women and passed a resolution for the protection and promotion of Human Rights of Women.

The Universal Declaration of Human Rights including other covenants and treatise lays down a standard code of Human Rights applicable to one and all, men and women regardless of race, caste and colour, sex, religion, language or place of birth. This is the common achievement of mankind for which it had been striving for centuries. These rights are inalienable and considered as foundations of freedom, justice, peace and development.

Human Rights in India

People throughout the world have always enjoyed certain types of freedoms and liberties having roots in the values and religions of the respective regions of our globe. This is true as well for the people of India. The internationalization of Human Rights embedded in the notion of respect and welfare of the people in general, highly influenced the Indian leadership and the social reformers. They were especially inspired by Bill of Rights of 1688, American Declaration of Independence of 1766, French Declaration of Independence 1789. On 10th of December 1948 when the Constitution of India was in making the UN General Assembly, adopted the Universal Declaration of Human Rights in 1948 which surely influenced the framing of Indian Constitution. Viewed from Indian standpoint, Human Rights have been synthesized into an integrated fabric by the preambular promises and various clauses of the Constitution.

The Constitution of India is a viable instrument of the Indian people's salvation and to secure all people's basic Human Rights is implicit from the Preamble which carries, Fundamental Rights, Directive Principles of State Policy, and various other provisions of the Constitution. The Preamble to the Constitution reads:

We, the People of India, having solemnly resolved to constitute India into a Sovereign, Socialist Secular, Democratic, Republic and to secure to all its citizens:

Justice, social, economic and political; Liberty of thought, expression, belief, faith and worship; Equality, of status and opportunity, and to promote among them all fraternity, assuring the dignity of the individual and the unity and integrity of the nation; In Our Constituent Assembly this twenty-sixth day of November 1949. Hereby Adopt, Enact and Give to Ourselves this Constitution.

The Preamble to the Constitution of India aimed to protect and promote the Human Rights of the people. Various objectives of the preamble find their expression in various provisions of the Fundamental Rights and the Directive

Principles of State Policy respectively. Many of the Human Rights in the Universal Declaration of Human Rights, 1948 and International Covenant on Civil and Political Rights, 1966 are guaranteed in part III of the Constitution of India.

Part III of the Constitution contains a long list of Fundamental Rights. They are classified under the following six groups:[5]

(a) Right to Equality (Articles 14-18)

(b) Right to Freedom (Articles 19-22)

(c) Right against Exploitation (Articles 23-24)

(d) Right to Freedom of Religion (Articles 25-28)

(e) Cultural and Educational Rights (Articles 29-30)

(f) Right to Constitutional Remedies (Articles 32-35)

These rights were deemed essential to protect the rights and liberties of the people against the abuse of the power delegated by them to their government. "These Fundamental Rights represent the basic values cherished by the people of this country (India) since the vedic times and they are calculated to protect the dignity of the individual and create conditions in which every human being can develop his personality to the fullest extent. They weave a pattern of guarantee on the basic structure of human rights and impose negative obligations on the state not to encroach on individual liberty in its various dimensions".[6] These rights are very fundamental for the attainment, by the individual, of his full development. The negation of these rights will keep his potentialities undeveloped. The object behind the inclusion of the Chapter of Fundamental Rights in Indian Constitution is to establish the Rule of law.

India's Constitution not only recognises the basic Human Rights, accepted/adopted by the international agencies/ authorities like UN and International Covenants, but has incorporated the same in itself (constitution) by positivization. A glance at the Fundamental Rights enshrined in Chapter III of Indian Constitution reveals lots of similarities with the provisions of Universal Declaration of Human Rights, 1948.

Provisions of Universal Declaration of Human Rights, 1948

Subject 1	*Indian Constitution* 2	*Universal Declaration of Human Rights* 3
(a) Sex, place of birth or any of them	Art 14 entitles to one and all equality before law property, birth or other status.	Art. 7-Sentence 2: All are entitled to equal protection against any discrimination in violation of this Declaration and against any incitement to such discrimination.
(b) Equality of opportunity in matters of public employment	Art. 16 (1): There shall be equality of opportunity for all citizens in matters relating to employment or appointment to any office under the State.	Art. 21 (2): Everyone has a right to equal access to public service in his country.
(c) Freedom of speech assembly, association etc.	Art. 19 (1) All citizens shall have the (a) Right to freedom of speech and expression (b) Right to assemble peaceably and without arms;	Art. 19: Everyone has the right to freedom of opinion and expression:.......... Art. 20 (1): Everyone has the right to freedom of peaceful assembly and association;
	(c) Right to form Unions and Associations	Art. 23 (4): Eveyone has a right to form and to join trade unions for the protection of his rights;
	(d) Right to move freely throughout the territory of India,	Art. 20 (2) No one may be compelled to belong to an association;
	(e) Right to reside and settle in any part of tho territory of India.	Art. 12 (1): Everyone has the right to freedom of movement and residence within the borders of each State.
(d) Protection in respect of conviction for offences	Art 20 (1): No person shall be convicted of any offence except for violation of law in force	Art 11 (2): No one shall be held guilty of any penal offence on account of any act or omission

Subject 1	Indian Constitution 2	Universal Declaration of Human Rights 3
	at the time of the commission of the act charged as an offence, nor be subjected to a penalty greater than that which might have been inflicted under the law in force at the time of the commission of the offence.	which may not constitute a penal offence, under national or international law, at the time when it was committed. Nor shall a heavier penalty be imposed than the one that was applicable at the time, the penal offence was committed.
(e)Protection of life and personal liberty.	Art. 21: No person shall be deprived of his life or personal liberty except according to procedure established by law.	Art. 3: Everyone has the right to life, liberty and security of person; Art. 9: No one shall be subjected to arbitrary arrest, detention or exile.
(f) Prohibition of traffic in human beings and forced labour.	Art. 23 (1): Traffic in human beings and "Begar" and other (similar forms of forced) labour are prohibited and any contravention of this provision shall be an offence punishable in accordance with law. Note : 'Begar' is a form of forced labour under which a person is compelled to work without remuneration.	Art. 4: No one shall be held in slavery or servitude; salvery or servitude shall be prohibited in all forms.
(g)Freedom of conscience and free profession, practice and propogation of religion.	Art. 25 (10) Subject to public order, morality and health and to the provisions of this part, all persons are equally entitled to freedom of conscience and right freely to profess, practice and propagate religion.	Art. 18: Everyone has the right to freedom of thought, conscience and religion; this right includes freedom to change his religion or belief, and freedom either alone or in community with others and in public or private,

Subject 1	*Indian Constitution* 2	*Universal Declaration of Human Rights* 3
		to change his religion or belief, and freedom either alone or in community with others and in public or private, to manifest his religion or belief in teaching, practice, worship and observance.
(h) Protection of interests of minorities.	Art. 29 (1): Any section of the citizens residing in the territory or any part thereof having a distinct language, script or culture of its own shall have the right to conserve the same.	Art. 22: Everyone, as a member of society, has the right to social security and is entitled to realisation through national effort and international cooperation and in accordance with the organisation and resources of each state.
(i) Right of minorities to establish and administer educational institutions.	Art. 30 (1): All minorities, whether based on religion or language, shall have the right to establish and administer educational institutions of their choice.	Art 26 (3): Parents have a prior right to choose the kind of education that shall be given to their children.
(j) Right to constitutional remedies.	Art. 32 (1): The right to move the Supreme Court by appropriate proceedings for the enforcement of rights conferred by this part is guaranteed. Note : 'By this part' refers to part-III Fundamental Rights.	Art. 8: Everyone has the right to an effective remedy by the tribunals for acts violating the fundamental rights granted to him by the constitution or by law.

Other than the inclusion a chapter on Fundamental Rights in Constitution, its framers also included Directive Principles of State Policy[7] contained in part IV of the Constitution which sets out the aims and objectives to be taken up by the states in the governance of the country.

This novel feature of Indian Constitution envisages a welfare state which has to promote prosperity and well being of the people. They lay down certain social, economic and political principles to be persued by various governments in India to promote the general welfare of the people[8] in consonance with the basic object of Human Rights. Read with preamble of Indian Constitution, they are in confirmity with the Articles 17 and 11 of the Covenant of Civil and Political Rights and the Covenant of Economic, Social and Cultural Rights respectively.

Though they are not enforceable by the courts, yet they have been declared to be fundamental in the governance of the country. Article-37 of the Constitution lays down that the Directive Principles are neverthless fundamental in the governance of the country and it shall be the duty of the state to apply these principles in making laws. These principles visualise a society in which every one will have the place of dignity and recognition of his identity. Moreover the Fundamental Rights will remain meaningless if the people who are to enjoy these rights are not free socially and economically. Thus, fundamental Rights are not anti-thesis of Directive Principles. They are meant to supplement one another. The Directive Principles prescribe the goal to be attained and Fundamental Rights laydown the means by which that goal is to be achieved. They are the conscience of the Constitution of India aiming at serving the cause of Human Rights in general as well as particular.

In post-independent India, a number of laws have been enacted for the general advancement of Indian people particularly Indian women. Laws favouring women have been legislated to give them rights and privileges equal with men to eliminate discrimination against them and removing hindrances coming in their way of self-realization and development. Among the enacted, many legislations with reference to woman, few significant ones are Act on Women's Legal Rights, 1952, the Suppression of Immoral Traffic in Women and Children Act, 1954; the Special Marriage Act, 1954; the Hindu Marriage and Divorce Act, 1956; Dowry Abolition Act, 1961; Indecent Representation of Women (Prohibition) Act, 1986; the Sati-Prevention Act,

1987. The Constitution of India is in accordance with the trend of modern democratic thought, the idea being to preserve that which is an indispensable condition of a free society, which ensures equal status to all—not only between men and men, women and women, but also between men and women. So the Constitution of India assures all among other thing dignity of individual. Human Rights are part and parcel of human dignity. Individual dignity can not be measured by single factor. It is the combination of all aspects : moral, economic, social and political etc. of human life.

Passing through various stages of socio-economic transformation, nature of man's rights and freedom has also undergone metamorphism and today the idea of 'Human Rights', has gained so much of momentum that it has encompassed all kinds of rights i.e. civil, social, economic, political within its purview, thus removing the centuries old divide between them. The concept of 'Human Rights' is anthropocentric—whatever adds to the welfare and dignity of human beings is an ingredient of it. Thus, providing a uniform code of rights, aiming at providing good and dignified life to a human being, transgressing all kinds of boundaries—territorial, physical, religious, gender, colour or race. A human being is simply a human being for the advocates of Human Rights entitled to a humane living. Humanity is the absolute yardstick and only language with the immediate as well as ultimate aim of providing atleast fundamental rights like right to life, liberty and property (enough for atleast subsistence), protecting human beings from any kind of discrimination, deprivation and exploitation. It applies equally to all the members of this globe irrespective of their origin, place of birth, territory, religion, caste or sex they belong to. They are the right which are inherent in our nature and without which we can not live as human beings. They allow us to fully develop and use our human qualities. They are based on mankinds increasing demand for a life in which the inherent dignity and worth of each human being will receive respect and protection.

Though constitutionally speaking, almost all the countries of the world today provide fundamental rights embodying various social, civil, political and economic rights to their citizens to enable them to lead a good, dignified life. But despite such provisicns, there is exploitation, deprivation, discrimination on a macro-level: a large number of people living under utter poverty, illiteracy and backwardness, without even two square meals a day, leaving aside the question of goodness and dignity; a large number of children without any childhood, working as labourers from the age of 7 or 8 years or indulging in beggary and other crimes. Majority of the half of the population of the world (i.e. females) do not have such words like freedom, rights, dignity and human worth in their vocabulary, amidst widespread gender discrimination and inequality. These are but a few examples highlighting the harsh realities of human life, the state of rights, freedoms and privileges available to the mankind for a good and dignified living.

The violation of the basic rights despite the fact that not various national and international enactments have been made relating to the protection of Human Rights by governmental authorities like bureaucracy, police and security forces, terrorists and other such criminals. The male section of the society (against women rights) make us realize that we have to march a lot on the path of even basic freedoms and rights of human beings

References

1. See for details - *Appendix-A.*
2. See for details, *Encydopedia of Human Rights,* Paramjit S. Jaswal and others, *Human Rights and Law,* APH Publishing Corporation, New Delhi, 1996.
3. *Ibid.*
4. See for details - *Appendix-B.*
5. See for details, J. N. Pandey, *Constitutional Law of India,* Central Law Agency, Allahabad, 1993.
6. *AIR* 1978 SC 597, p. 619.
7. See for details, J. N. Pandey, *Constitutional Law of India,* Central Law Agency, Allahabad, 1993.
8. Granville Austin, *Cornerstone of a Nation* (Indian Constitution), p. 75.

2

Women and Human Rights

The question of Human Rights with its emphasis on the rights of women has become a dominant agenda of international society. However, it is equally paradoxical to note that the growing assertion of rights of women continues to be coincided with the growing violence of all kinds against them. Hence, the fundamental question is, how to resolve this contradiction of so called 'Modern Society'. It is a matter of fact that the various UN declarations, declarations of other women bodies, women NGOS and the series of legislations formulated in the past by the parliament of various countries has not fundamentally improved socio-economic and political status of women in the society. Women continues to be on the periphery in the society and are being further marginalised by the process of what is called 'Globalisation' particularly in the developing countries. It seems that the growing incidence of violence and other kinds of abuses against women has two interrelated causative factors—

Firstly, the growing peripherisation of women emanates from the nature of development.

Secondly, the massive propaganda of consumerist ideology with sexual overtones sponsored by global capital is increasingly reducing the woman to the status of mere a commodity to be used like many other consumerable items.

The benefit of developmental process has not accrued to women in a sense of investing and legalising her share in the property and also in the production process. The economic enhancement of women essentially implies what is called the freedom to exercise choice. Unfortunately no thrust from any quarter or forum at any level-local, national and international-has been paid to this fundamental aspect of women's development. That is why one sees that no serious call has been made by votaries of women rights to fight the feudal and patriarchal culture of the society which is the root cause of backwardness. This speaks why the various legislations have failed to ameliorate the condition of women.

Further, women are becoming much more vulnerable because of growing assertion of consumerist ideology. For an 'alienated potential individual' in a market society women becomes a soft target. The tendency to acquire an appropriate consumerist item create the conditions which shapes the man's behaviour towards women. A significant feature of consumerist society is the lust for material gains marked by cut-throat-competition for the same. Consequently the gainers are few handful of people and rest which constitute the majority are the deprived lot. But it is the woman who becomes the victim of the frustration emerging out of material deprivation. This paves way for all kinds of atrocities ranging from gender discrimination, deprivation to exploitation (physical, mental, sexual, economic, social etc.) and sexual abuses of all kinds. Consumerism has reduced woman to an almost 'use' and 'throw' status. She is no more a 'human being' but merely a 'commodity'.

Though constituting half the population of the world and often referred to as the 'Better half of Man', women, in fact have the worst deal at the hands of society, even today. They are physically and sexually abused and exploited; denied a role in the governance; denied equal wages and largely treated as an appendage of man, when old/widowed in some cases discarded and disregarded even by the family. Whatever may be the caste/religion/nation or state-women as a community is the most backward, ill-treated and exploited one.

Women in most of the countries are subjected to discriminatory restrictions, deprived of their fundamental freedom regarding voting, marriage, travel, property ownership and inheritance, custody of children, citizenship and court testimony. Besides there is sex-based discrimination in access to education, employment, health care, financial services etc. Violence against them takes many forms but is universal. The UN development programmes, Annual Human Development Report commented that "in no society are women secure or treated as equal to men. Personal insecurity shadows them from cradle to grave. From childhood through adulthood they are abused because of their gender".[1] Sexual harassment which is defined as unwelcome, sexually determined behaviour (whether directly or by implication) as physical contact and advances, a demand or request for sexual favours, sexually coloured remarks; showing pornography, any other unwelcome physical, verbal or non-verbal conduct of sexual nature is a common problem being faced by the working women as well as female students throughout the world. According to a survey conducted by a women group, about 60 per cent of its respondents who were working women had faced sexual harassment at the work place while 35 per cent of female students said they faced such harassment at school or college.[2] Coming to the reproductive health rights which came into limelight because of the World Conferences on Population and Development held in Cairo in 1994 and on Women held in Beijing in 1995, we are still far behind. The position of women in this regard is much pathetic in Asia and Africa. Moreover, ignorance, unawareness and illiteracy about their rights on the part of women and non-recognition of reproductive rights as Human Rights are the chief culprits. But lot in adequacies persist in legal set up also like inequality in the rights of women to marry and divorce as men and the denial of right to inheritance particularly if they are widows.

Women's issue highlights the deprivation and discriminations to which they are subjected to in all the societies. This deprivation which is merely on the basis of sex, permitted to a large part on the arbitrary division of male-female roles in the society. Despite the productive contributions of the life and wealth of the nation, they are subjected to discrimination in every walk of life; she is relegated to the level of 'passive' participants rather than the 'active' one in all activities.[3] Gender bias, in it's various forms, prevents millions of women from obtaining education, health services, child-care and legal status needed to escape poverty etc. Today women comprise 66 per cent of the world's illiterates and 70 per cent of the world's poor. Deep rooted socio-religious traditions have further created bottlenecks in their progress to great extent.

Coming to the state of Indian woman we will find that undoubtedly Indian woman is one of the most backward in the world. She is also among the most illiterate. Because of the patriarchal mindset she is not equal even in the womb, she is violated as foetus because of her sex. In Indian homes, female child recognised as 'Parayadhan' gets less food, less education, lesser share of everything. Not only discrimination but she also faces problems of domestic violence where woman day after day is beaten, harassed and attacked by her own man. The problem of battered women remains a hidden crime because most of the cases go unreported as the crime is done within the four walls of home. The victims most of the time fear social stigma. Fear of living, family prestige, apprehension about their own future and that of the children, financial problems and fear of divorce are also equally important factors allowing the exploiters a safe escape and also encourage further such crimes, called domestic violence including wife-battering, torture for dowry, sexual perversion and the forms which may range from minor burning to fractures, throwing acid and even murder. Female foeticide latest in the series of crimes against women, not only involves the crime of killing a girl child before she is born but also attacking the very dignity of womanhood i.e. woman as a gender is unwanted on this earth. It is because of deep rooted psyche that girl is a liability and boy is an asset. This factor was earlier responsible for an inhuman practice, like female infanticide and now to female foeticide.

Reducing woman to a sex object is largely rooted in male psyche responsible for a range of crimes from eveteasing, disgusting and insulting a woman, sexual harassment, pornographic and obscene representation of females, to physical molestation, rape and illegal trafficking.

Though it is worthless to discuss the issue of dignity of woman against such a gloomy scenario where even the 'survival' or existence of woman is at stake. Dignity is attached to the identity of a human being as a person; when a human being does not enjoy the right to be a person; dignity does not exist at all. While talking about the Human Rights 'human' aspect of the right has to be emphasized. If a right is not effective in helping a human being to lead his/her life in a humanly manner or if it does not give him/her the right to live a life of dignity, it is not worthwhile.

By nature women are considered inferior to males, but it is our societal and religious setup that has relegated them to such an inferior status resulting in widespread gender discrimination and deprivation. Despite their enormous contribution to family income, they are considered an unproductive element of economy as well as family; because of gender discrimination women are deprived of basic education, health, child care as well as legal rights and freedoms, which are no significant things if we take an account of the nature and extent of crimes committed against women like rape, trafficking in women and prostitution, infanticide and foeticide, sexual harassment etc. Besides socio-religious factors, illiteracy and poverty are two major causes of prevailing gender discrimination and various kinds of cruelties and criminalities committed against women, throughout the world, not only in India.

Women in India from the days of Manu, have been suppressed and oppressed. They have been subjected to various kinds of cruelties throughout the history. And even today, in the face of a series of laws for the advancement of women, they are subjugated and exploited. Their subjugation and exploitation is primarily being done in the name of safeguarding the personal laws. Personal laws in India which are the product of socio-religious set up of the country are highly discriminatory in nature, as far as women are concerned. It will be appropriate to discuss them in brief here.

Personal Laws

Personal laws[4] deal with marriage and divorce, maintenance, guardianship, adoption, inheritance and succession, ownership of property etc, These laws are basically divided along religious lines in India, irrespective of their religious basis. Thus Hindus are governed by the Hindu Marriage Act, 1955; the Hindu Succession Act, 1956; the Hindu Guardianship and Minority Act, 1956; and the Hindu Adoption and Maintenance Act, 1956. Muslims are governed by the Shartiat Act, 1937; the Muslim Women's (Protection of Right on Divorce) Act, 1986; and Uncodified Muslim Personal Laws. Christians are governed by the Christian Marriage Act, 1972; the Indian Divorce Act, 1869, and the Indian Succession Act, 1925. The Parsees are governed by the Parsi Marriage and Divorce Act, 1936.

The main characteristic of all these personal laws is that they are largely anti-women and blatantly discriminatory especially in their implementation. Apart from unequal treatment meted out to them within each community, these laws subject them to varying degrees of discrimination and exploitation. For example, while a Hindu, Christian and Parsi wife can sue her husband for bigamy, a Muslim woman cannot because Muslim personal law allows a Muslim man to have four wives at a time. Even in those cases where the law is codified, as among Hindus, and accords equality, wide gap exists in legal prescriptions and societal acceptance. The girl's consent to marriage is generally never sought or obtained. In all family matters, she is expected to allow her husband to take all decisions. Even though she has a remunerative job, the choice relating to "matrimonial home" is the proregative of the husband though there have been new welcome judicial developments in this direction.

In the matter of inheritance, while the Hindu Succession Act, 1956 maintains the equality of the sexes in general and confers right of inheritance on female heirs (Section 8), it contains several retrogressive features to the detriment of the women. By virtue of Article 4(2), "laws providing for the prevention of fragmentation of agricultural holding" have been exempted from the application of the Act. This means that in the name of "prevention of fragmentation of agricultural land" a Hindu woman could be deprived of her right to property. Further, a restriction on her right to demand partition is imposed by Section 23, that is, if a Hindu dies, intestate his female heir cannot claim partition of the dwelling house untill the male heirs choose to divide their respective shares therein, and till then the female heir is entitled to a right of residence only. Where the female heir is daughter, she has a right of residence in the dwelling house only if she is unmarried or has been deserted by or separated from her husband or is a widow. The Act also provides that if a female Hindu dies intestate without leaving behind children or husband, her property will devolve on her husband's heirs, except the property inherited from her parents, which in the absence of a son or a daughter or their-children, will devolve on the heirs of her father.

The Hindu Guardianship and Minority Act, 1956 also accepts the father as the natural guardian of the child, and only in his absence, the mother can be the natural guardian. The mother can have the custody of the minor child who has not completed the age of five years, a provision which in itself is inhuman and unequal.

The Muslim personal law requires a bit of pruning to make it conform to the concept of equality. The polygamy practice is at variance with other personal laws. Regarding divorce, the Dissolution of Muslim Marriage Act, 1939 has undoubtedly ameliorated the conditions of Muslim women. However, the retention of the provision of unilateral divorce by pronouncing *Talaq* by the husband under the Muslim law, together with the prevailing practice of polygamy undermines severly the dignity and the status of woman. After the passing of the Muslim Women's (Protection of Rights and Divorce) Act, 1986 in the wake of Shah Bano's case[5] the Muslim woman's right to seek maintenance from her husband under Sections 125-127 of the Criminal Procedure

Code has been severely curtailed in comparison with other Indian women. The Act restricts the right of maintenance only to the *iddat* period (about three months) after divorce and stipulates that thereafter her own family and the Waqf Board would be responsible for her maintenance. In the matter of inheritance, though she has the right to inherit, she is treated unequal to her male counterpart. For instance, a son will take double the share of the daughter and a brother will take double the share of the sister. But this is in accordance with the Shariat. There is no provision for adoption under the Muslim law. Earlier attempts to have an Indian Adoption Act failed because of the opposition of the Muslims to such optional laws governing adoption. Any attempt to change the Muslim law is considered to be an interference in the religious matters and contrary to the Shariat.

The Christian and the Parsi laws of marriage and divorce do not reveal any major disparity in the status of men and women. But the law is found to be demonstrably inadequate where cruelty alone is not a ground for divorce under the Indian Divorce Act, 1869 but is a ground only for judicial separation, unless accompanied by another ground for divorce. This Act, besides being archaic, obviously is discriminatory against women. The inhuman treatment is meted out to a wife who is subjected to cruel behaviour of the husband and yet cannot get divorce. Divorce by mutual consent is not permissible under the Indian Divorce Act, 1869. The Act recognises only adultery as a ground for divorce for men. Wife can ask for divorce only if the husband has changed his religion (a Christian husband cannot seek divorce on wife's conversion to another religion) and married another woman or has been guilty of adultery along with bigamy or rape, sodomy, bestiality, cruelty or desertion. Thus, provisions of the Act clearly discriminate against women on the grounds of sex alone.[6] The Parsi Marriage and Divorce Act 1939 governs the Parsees. But in the matter of inheritance, the Indian Succession Act, 1925 accords complete equality among Christians, and under the Parsi law son gets the share of the daughter. Personal Laws of every community are essentially anti-women.

In such a scenario where the condition of Indian woman is pathetic it is pertinent here to analyse the various constitutional and other provisions which protect and promote the basic rights of Indian women. Indian Constitution is an instrument which guarantees to all the citizens of India certain basic Human Rights implicit from the Preambular promises, Fundamental Rights and Directive Principles of State Policy.

Constitutional Provisions Fundamental Rights

Right to Equality *(Articles 14-18)*

The Constitution of India enunciates the general principle of right to equality and prohibits the state from denying to any person equality before the law or the equal protection of the law. Articles 14 to 18 of the Constitution guarantees the right to equality to every citizen of India. Article 14 embodies the general principles of equality before law and prohibits unreasonable discrimination between persons. The succeeding Articles 15,16,17 and 18 lay down specific application of the general rules laid down in Article 14. Article 15 prohibits the discrimination on grounds of religion, race, caste, sex or place of birth. Article 16 guarantees equality of opportunity in matter's of public employment. Article 17 abolishes untouchability and Article 18 abolishes title. The guardian of the Indian Constitution, the Supreme Court of India has always been the champion in maintaining and elaborating the concept of equality of status. Hostile discrimination against women has always been struck down by the Supreme Court of India from time to time because ----- "since sex like race and national origin is an immutable characteristic determined solely by accident of birth, the imposition of special disability upon the member of their sex (female) would seem to violate the basic concept of our system that legal burdens should bear some relationship to individual responsibility".[7] Though Article 14 of the Constitution prohibits class legislation but permits reasonable classification. The Supreme Court declared that woman as a class were different from men as a class.[8] Having inview the object of the legislation, women can be treated as a class and special laws can be made in their favour. Accordingly various provisions have been declared valid where women have been given special treatment.

Right to Freedom *(Articles 19-22)*

Personal liberty is the most important of all Fundamental Rights. Articles 19 to 22 deal with different aspect of this basic right. These four Articles concerning personal liberties are the backbone of the chapter on Fundamental Rights. The foremost among these are the six basic rights in the nature of freedoms guaranteed to the Indian citizens by Article 19 of the Constitution. These six freedoms are as follows:

(a) Freedom of Speech and Expression,

(b) Freedom of Assembly,

(c) Freedom to Form Associations,

(d) Freedom of Movement,

(e) Freedom to Reside and to Settle,

(f) Freedom of Profession, Occupation, Trade or Business.

These freedoms are, however not absolute because absolute freedom can not be guaranteed by any state. Any right which is injurious to the community as a whole can not be protected. This is based on the principle that for liberty of one must not offend the liberty of others. However, the restrictions which may be imposed by the state must be reasonable restrictions.

Right Against Exploitation *(Articles 23-24)*

Article 23 of the Constitution prohibits traffic in human being and beggar and other similar forms of forced labour. Traffic in human being means selling and buying men and women like goods and includes immoral traffic in women and children for immoral or other purposes.[9] This article protects the individual not only against the state but also against private citizens. It imposes an obligation on the state to undertake measures to abolish the evils of traffic in human beings and forms of forced labour wherever they are found. Article 24 of the Constitution prohibits the employment of children below 14 years of age in factories and hazardous employment. This Article however, does not prohibit their employment in any harmless work.

Right to Freedom of Religion *(Articles 25-28)*

Article 25 (1) of the Constitution guarantees to every person the freedom of conscience and the right to profess, practice and propagate religion. This right like other rights guaranteed by the Constitution is not absolute. This right is subject to public order, morality and health and to the other provision of the Chapter III of the Constitution. The state is empowered by law under sub-clauses (a) and (b) and clause (2) of the Article 25 (a) to regulate or restrict any economic, financial, political or other activity which may be associated with religious practice; (b) to provide for (i) social welfare and reform, and (ii) to throw open Hindu religious institutions of public character to all classes and sections of Hindus.

Article 26 of the Constitution says that every religious demonstration of any section of it shall have the following rights subject to the public order, morality and health:

(a) to establish and maintain institutions for religious and charitable purposes,

(b) to manage its own affairs in matters of religion,

(c) to own and acquire moveable and immoveable property,

(d) to administer such property in accordance with law.

The right guaranteed by Article 26 is not an individual right like the one guaranteed by Article 25. It is a right of an organised body.

Article 27 provides that no person shall be compelled to pay any tax for the promotion or maintenance of any particular religion or religious denominations. This Article emphasises the secular character of the state. Article 28 says no religious instruction shall be imparted in any educational institution wholly maintained out of the state fund. However this clause shall not apply to an educational institution which is administered by the state, but has been established under any endowment or trust which requires that religious instruction shall be imparted in the institution.

Cultural and Educational Rights *(Articles 29-30)*

Article 29 (1) guarantees to any section of the citizens residing in any part of India having a distinct language, script or culture of its own, the right to conserve the same i.e language, script or culture. A minority community can preserve its language, script or culture by or through educational institutions. Therefore, the right to establish and maintain institutions of their choice is a necessary concomitant to the right to preserve its distinctive langauge, script or culture. Article 30 (1) of the Constitution guarantees this right to them (minorities) based either on religion or language. This right is subject to the clause (2) of Article 29, which says no citizen shall be denied admission into any educational institutions maintained by the state, or receiving aid out of state fund on grounds only of religion race, caste, language, or any of them. The right conferred on the religious and linguistic minorities to administer educational institutions of their choice is not absolute. This right is not free from regulation.

Right to Constitutional Remedies *(Articles 32-35)*

Right to constitutional remedies "is the very soul of the Constitution and the very heart of it".[10] It is true that a declaration of Fundamental Rights is meaningless in the absence of an effective machinery to enforce them. It is the remedy which makes a right, a right in reality. If there is no remedy there is no right at all.

Article 32 of the Constitution which itself is a Fundamental Right provides for an effective remedy for the enforcement of other Fundamental Rights. Not only this, Article 226 of the Constitution also empowers all the High Courts of India to issue the writs for the enforcement of Fundamental Rights.

Article 32(1) guarantees the right to move to Supreme Court by appropriate proceedings for the enforcement of the Fundamental Rights. Clause (2) of the Article confers power on the Supreme Court to issue appropriate directions or orders or writs. Under this Article the Supreme Court's power to enforce Fundamental Rights is widest. However, it is guaranteed by the Constitution that whenever there is violation of Fundamental Rights any person can move to the court for an appropriate remedy, this right is restricted and can also be abrogated in certain situations according to Articles 33 and 34.

Directive Principles of State Policy

Besides the Fundamental Rights, the Directive Principles of State Policy set out the aims and objectives to be taken up by the states in the governance of the country. The Directive Principles of State Policy (Articles 36-51) seek to secure to all the citizens of India social, economic and political justice. Though these principles[11] are not enforceable by court, they, no doubt, impose a duty on the state to establish a welfare state. Article 38 specially requires the state to direct its policy towards securing the following objectives:

(a) Equal right of men and women to adequate means of livelihood,

(b) Distribution of ownership and control of the meterial resources of the community for the general welfare,

(c) To ensure that the economic system should not result in concentration of wealth and means of production to the common detriment,

(d) Equal pay for equal work for both men and women,

(e) To protect health and strength of workers and tender age of children to ensure that they are not forced by economic necessity to enter a vocations unsuited to their age or strength,

(f) That children are given opportunities and facilities to develop in a healthy manner and in conditions of freedom and dignity and that childhood and

dignity and that childhood and youth are protected against exploitation and against moral and material abandonment.

(g) The Directive Principles also impose a duty upon the state under Article 44 to secure for the citizens of India a uniform civil code throughout the territory of India.

Besides this, there are various other objectives laid down by the Directive Principles of State Policy to secure them. Pursuant to these principles, many Acts have been passed by the state to improve general welfare of the people of India particularly the women. Some gender specific legislations are : The Special Marriage Act, 1954; The Marriage Law (Amendment) Act, 1976; The Dowry Prohibition Act, 1961; Maternity Benefit Act, 1961; Equal Remuneration Act, 1976; Family Courts Act, 1984; The Indecent Representation of Women (Prohibition) Act, 1986; The Commission of Sati (Prevention) Act, 1987; The National Commission for Women Act, 1990. These enactments have, no doubt, improved the status of women but much more is needed to ameliorate the general betterment of women.

Other than the Constitutional provisions available to the Indian women, the Indian Penal Code and the Criminal Procedure Code provide for the gender specific protection of woman. The Indian Penal Code, in general, does not make any distinction on the basis of sex. It is uniformally applicable to all. However, looking to the social conditions and norms prevailing in the Indian Society the Penal Code has provided special provisions which afford protections to woman who could be a victim of the offences relating to her sex. For example, the offence of adultery under Section 497 of Indian Penal Code which provides that a women who has voluntarily participated in the offence of adultery can not be punished. There are number of Sections of Indian Penal Code which provide for the special protection to women. Like Indian Penal Code the Criminal Procedure Code also provides some provisions in favour of women. These special provisions protect the weaker lot of the society. There are number of Sections like Section 47(2), Section 51(2), Section 64, Sections 1 & 5 etc. which protect women.

The full and non-discriminatory realization of Human Rights is indispensable to the process of democracy and sustainable development. Though Indian Constitution provides for Right to Constitutional Remedies to redress Human Rights grievances and violations or Fundamental Rights, the need was felt that some independent machinery falling outside the control of administration, for better protection of the Human Rights of the people must be created. It is in this regard that the Protection of Human Rights Act, 1993 was enacted in India. Accordingly, the National Human Rights Commission was constituted under the Protection of Human Rights Act, 1993 for the speedy protection of Human Rights.

The Constitution of India provides for the equal status of all. It ensures to the Indian women equal rights and privileges with men, eliminates discrimination against them, abolishes inequality between sexes and removes external barriers coming in self-realization and development. Not only this, it also provides for the special enactment of laws favouring women under Article 14. Though much more has been achieved and much more is to be achieved to eliminate the political, economic and social disparities which continue to exist in Indian society disfavouring the women.

The Constitution of India which guarantees right to one and all without discriminating among them suffers from a discrepancy. Article 25 of the Constitution which allows freedom of religion has been interpreted to mean that religious customs, even if blatantly discriminating against women, will take precedence over other civil laws particularly in two areas relating to marriage and the family structure and the ownership of the property-inheritance.

To over come the existing disparity in treatment of women from different communities and to give effect to the equality concept under personal laws, the enactment of a uniform civil code, as directed under Article 44 of the Constitution will be a desired step. This is also required to fulfil India's commitment under the Discrimination against Women Convention, 1979 which mandates states to accord complete equality on matters of marriage, divorce, inheritance, ownership etc. But the Government of India has not done much so far to fulfil its constitutional or treaty obligations, inspite of the judical eloquence to enact such a code. In the Shah Bano[12] case the Supreme Court expressed its deep regret that Article 44 of the Constitution has remained a dead letter. It observed that "there is no evidence of any official activity for framing a common civil code for the country" and that a beginning has to be made if the Constitution is to have any meaning. The Supreme Court once again asked the Government in May 95 to take a fresh look at Article 44 and has directed it to ask the Law Commission to draft a comprehensive legislation incorporating the present day concept of Human Rights for women in consultation with the Minorities Commission.[13]

The Supreme Court further stated that Article 44 had sought to "divest religion from social relations and personal laws." The personal laws are to operate under the authority of legislation and not of the religion, and they can be superseded or supplemented by a uniform civil code. But we are still far behind on the path of uniform civil code or some thing like that to relieve the women from the clause of partriarchal set-up which discriminates on the basis of sex contrary, the basic principle of non-discrimination laid down by the Indian Constitution.

Despite so much of legal protection and liabilities on the part of government gender justice appears to be a myth in India. Women are still the sufferer of gender discrimination both in private as well as public life. They suffer discrimination, deprivation and exploitation for being women. Because of gender discrimination they are the poorest, illiterate, and most miserable section of all castes as well as communities, suffering a number of atrocities like dowry-deaths, criminalities like rape, sexual harassment, physical and mental torture etc, which are on an increase, despite the high place given to 'Gender Justice' in Indian Constitution. There is no dearth of laws in this regard, even then Indian women are discriminated socially, economically, politically and culturally/religiously.

References

1. *Nation and the World*, May 1, 1998, pp. 12-19.
2. *Ibid.*
3. "The Realization of the Right in Development" , *UN Document HR/ PVB/91, p. 37.*
4. For details see A.M. Bhattacharjee, *Hindu Law and the Constitution*, Eastern Law House, New Delhi, 1994; Asaf A Fyzee, *Outlines of Mohammadan Law*, Oxford University Press, Delhi, 1993; Anjani Kant, *Women and Law*, APH Publishing Corporation, New Delhi, 1997.
5. Md. Ahmad Khan Vs Shah Bano, *AIR*, 1995, p. 945.
6. *Times of India*, June 6, 1995, p. 11.
7. Sharron A. Frontiero Vs Elliot L. Richardson, 1973, *36 LED*, 2583.
8. Kaur Singh Vs Jaggar Singh, *AIR*, 1961, Punjab, p. 489.
9. Raj Bahabur Vs Legal Remembrances, *AIR*, 1953, Calcutta, p. 522.
10. *CAD*, Vol. VII, p. 953.
11. See for details, J.N. Pandey, Constitutional Law of India, Central Law Agency, Allahabad, 1993.
12. Md. Ahmad Khan Vs Shah Bano, *AIR*, 1995, p. 945.
13. Sarla Mudgal, President, Kalyani and others Vs Union of India, 1995 (3) *SCALE 286*, p. 299.

3

Crimes Against Women

A woman in India who is worshipped as Lakshami (Goddess of Wealth), Saraswati (Goddess of Learning), Kali and Durga (Goddess of Power and Strength) is also subjected to different kinds of cruelties. She is subjected to criminal assault every 54 minutes, a molestation takes place every 26 minutes, a dowry related death every 102 minutes, kidnapping and abduction every 43 minutes and an act of eve teasing every 51 minutes. Official figures show that crime against women in 1996 has increased by 5.9 per cent and 7.5 per cent over the last two years. The National Crimes Record Bureau has indicated that incidence of rape cases and dowry-death cases during 1996 over 1995 reported and increase of 7.9 per cent and 8.3 per cent respectively. There have been 11,259 dowry related murders officially registered in the last 3 years. Despite a legislation, foeticide is routinely performed, using amniocentesis and ultrasound procedures to preselect boys and abort female foetuses. One study shows that of the 8000 abortions performed at a particular clinic, most of were female foetuses.[1] These crimes, despite the fact that there are laws to protect women, are on the rise. They have rather become the order of the day. The fact is that a woman in India suffers gender violence all through her life. It could be in the nature of sex-selective abortions, female foeticide, child marriage, prostitution, domestic violence, dowry exploitation and deaths, sexual offences and harassment, employment discrimination and abuse of widows. Some of them are analysed here in context of crime specific laws to prevent them. The analysis is intended to focuss on the discrepancies in laws.

Dowry

The evil of dowry in Indian society is widespread throughout its territory, among all the communities. The dowry system is not original to the Hindu society, it was something unknown to Vedic society. The dowry system in Vedic times was associated with the marriage as a daan or gift—gift to be given to son-in-law at the time of marriage. Earlier it was a voluntary act made out of love and affection which later on assumed the frightening name of dowry for the obtaining of which compulsion, coercion, and force began to be used ultimately resulting into bargaining of marriages.

In the contemporary Indian society, dowry has assumed all the features of market transactions, making marriage a trade, an opportunity for making maximum possible material gains. It results in the economic exploitation of girl's parents, making marriage a big problem and cause of frustration among girls who either don't get married at all or married at much later age. This makes a girl an unwanted person in the family thus encouraging practices like female foeticide.

The practice of dowry is completely anti-women. It reduces women to a commodity, a source of income for the groom and his family and an economic liability for the bride's parents. At times even a handsome dowry, does not ensure a happy and secure life for the girl in matrimonial home. The evil of dowry and the related treatment is so harsh that women can not consider herself a human being. The evil of dowry has now assumed menacing proportions. It is very common these days that brides, on account of their failure to bring the promised or expected dowry are beaten-up, kept without food for days together locked up in dingy rooms, tortured physically and mentally, strangulated, burnt alive or led to commit sucide.

The Indian Parliament enacted a Dowry Prohibition Act[2] in 1961 with a view to eradicate the social evil of dowry. This Act, did not prove effective and the evil of dowry continued to reign supreme. Several Indian states amended the Dowry Prohibition Act, 1961 to provide it more teeths but the dowry menace continued to persist. The Government of India referred the whole matter for consideration by a Joint Committee of both the Houses of Parliament. The Committee went into the whole matter in great depth and opined in its report of 1982 that for the failure of Dowry Prohibition Act, 1961 there are two reasons: first, the explanation to Section 2 of the Act excludes all presents (whether given in cash or kind) from the definition of dowry unless the same were given in consideration of marriage and it is almost impossible to prove that gifts or presents given at, before, or after the marriage were in consideration of marriage. Since no giver of the present will ever come forward to say that he gave the same in consideration of marriage, as giving of dowry is as much an offence as taking it. Secondly, the Act has no effective enforcement instrumentality. No court can take cognizance of a dowry crime except on a complaint made by a person within one year from the date of the commission of dowry offence. It is unrealistic to expect the bride or bride's parents or other relations to lodge a complaint. The parents are usually the victims of dowry. They are reluctant to come forward because of the apprehension that this act may lead to the victimization of their daughter. Some of the recommendations of the Joint Parliamentary Committee were accepted by the Parliament which are incorporated into the Dowry Prohibition (Amendment) Act, 1984 and 1986.

Dowry is now defined as any property or valuable security given or agreed to be given directly or indirectly (a) by one party to the marriage to the other party to marriage or (b) by parents of either party to the marriage or by any other person to either party to the marriage or to any other person at or before or at any time after the marriage in connection with the marriage of said parties. The Act uses the word dowry in two senses: What is given by bride's parents to either bridegroom or their daughter or by the parents of bride-groom to him or their daughter-in-law (bride). This amended definition has broadened the meaning of dowry but it does not include the wedding presents in its purview. We can say that whatever does not constitute wedding presents constitute dowry. This leaves ample room for the abuse of law.

Furthermore, taking or giving of dowry or abetting to give dowry or abetting to take dowry continue to be offences even after the amendment of the Act. The Joint Parliamentary Committee on Dowry was of the opinion that the giver of the dowry should not be treated as an offender as he is more a victim than an offender. It further opined that when the giver of the dowry is considered to be as much an offender as the taker of the dowry, the prosecution of the taker or demander of dowry becomes difficult. When both the giver and taker of dowry are punishable under the Act, no giver will venture out to make a complaint. Dowry Prohibition Law is a peculiar law which considers both the committer of the offence as well as against whom the offence has been committed as offender. This peculiarity of the Act exercises great restrain on the parents of bride not to seek the help of law unless the situations force them to do so. Despite the fact that the various efforts have been made by the governments in India to deal with the problem of dowry the evil of dowry continues to grow. Moreover, the dowry related offences take place within the four-walls of a house where no eye witness is available, other than the inmates who are themselves offender, to prove the crime which leads to acquital in most cases. There is not even two per cent convictions.[3]

Though the dowry is a social problem which needs to be controlled socially by stepping up anti-dowry publicity and awareness. The Dowry Prohibition Act has been amended from time to time but the unscrupulous manage to escape the clutches of law, it is therefore, essential to amend the law to give it more teeths to tackle the evil of dowry more effectively. The bride's parents who are generally exploited or forced to give dowry to either groom or his parents are themselves the victims of dowry, they shall not be held as offender of the crime so that they may come forward to report to the police the dowry related crimes against their daughters.

Sexual Offences

There are many situations of violence against women. And one of most extreme forms of such violence is rape.

It is such a heinous crime that it is destructive of the whole personality of the victim. Though this crime is committed against women every where on this planet, Indian records are unabashedly shameful. According to the statistics of the National Crime Records Bureau there has been an increase of 431 per cent in the number of rapes since 1971. The rate of increase in the number of rapes is far in excess of the general increase in crime as the incidence of murders are reported to have increased only by 254 per cent from 1953 to 1994. What is ironical is that despite the laws[4] such an alarming increase in the crimes against women is on the increase.

Rape is covered under Section 376 of Indian Penal Code. Under this Section if a women is compelled to submit to sexual intercourse without her consent, she may be entitled to redress from the law. For such a redressal however, it is necessary for a women to prove that she was not a consenting party to the intercourse, that intercourse did occur, that she did not by her manner of dress, or any other way, invite intercourse, that she is a women of good character, and that she did not resist rape under consideration of fear or because she was aware that resistance would incite the rapist to further violence and was considered to have cooperated. Similarly it is not possible under the law for a prostitute to be raped. Since she is not a women of good character on this account many incidence of criminal assault are not even reported. Moreover in situations of rape, social pressures affect the process of redressal. The outcome of it is that woman is intimidated by the stigma of unchastity and, therefore, hesitate to report the incidence of rape which results into the protection and encouragement of the rapists. One who dares to complaint faces the biases of the social and legal system right from the police investigation to the judicial process, the onus is her to prove the rape. Moreover, very rarely a conviction is carried through. Despite the fact that many incidence of rapes do not come to light yet there is a shockingly alarming increase in the sexual offences against the women.

According to the existing law the punishment provided is a minimum of seven years imprisonment in rape as such and a minimum of ten years for gang rape, custodial rape of minors with provision of a lesser sentence at the discretion of the court for adequate and special reasons to be mentioned in the judgement. This provision has been used to reduce the sentences on the ground of the sexual antecedents of the victim. A draft bill on sexual offences was prepared by the National Commission for Women which proposed a number of amendments including non-citation of the sexual antecedents of the rape victim during the course of trial. Truthfully speaking woman's character does not abrogate her rights over her body, so the character or reputation of the victim has no bearing on relevance either in the matter of adjudging the guilt of the accused or imposing punishment under Section 376.[5]

The Supreme Court of India made the following observation about the defects in the present system:[6]

"Firstly, complaints are handled roughly and are not given such attention as is warranted. The victims, more often not are humiliated by the police. The victims have invariably found rape trials a traumatic experience. The experience of giving evidence in court has been negative and destructive. The victims often say, they considered the ordeal to be even worse than the rape itself. Undoubtedly, the court proceeding added to and prolonged the psychological stress they had to suffer as a result of the rape itself". Moreover, the Hon'ble Court also laid down the following broad parameters in assisting the victims of rape:

1. The complainants of sexual assault cases should be provided with legal representation. It is important to have someone who is well acquainted with the criminal justice system. The role of the victim's advocate would not only explain to the victim the nature of the proceedings, to prepare her for the case and to assist her in the police station and in court, but to provide her with guidance as to how she might obtain help of a different nature from other agencies, for example mind counselling or medical assistance. It is important

to secure continuity of assistance by ensuring that the same person who looked after the complainant's interest in the police station represent her till the end of the case.

2. Legal assistance will have to be provided at the police station since the victim of sexual assault might very well be in a distressed state upon arrival at the police station, the guidance and support of a lawyer at this stage whilst she was being questioned would be of great assistance to her.
3. The police should be under duty to inform the victim of her right to representation before any questions were asked of her and that the police report should state the victim was so informed.
4. A list of advocates willing to act in these cases should be kept at the police station for victims who did not have a particular lawyer in mind or whose own lawyer was unavailable.
5. The advocate shall be appointed by the court, upon application by the police at the earliest convenient moment, but in order to ensure that victims were questioned without undue delay, advocates would be authorised to act at the police station before leave of the court was sought or obtained.
6. In all rape trials anonymity of the victim must be maintained, as far as necessary.
7. It is necessary having regard to the Directive Principles contained under Article 38(1) of the Constitution of India to set up Criminal Injuries Compensation Board. Rape victims frequently incur substantial financial loss. Some, for example are too traumatised to continue in employment.
8. Compensation for victims shall be awarded by the court on conviction of the offender and by the Criminal Injuries Compensation Board whether or not a conviction has taken place. The Board will take into account pain, suffering and shock as well as loss of earnings due to pregnancy and the expenses of child birth if this

occurred as a result of the rape[7]. "Interim compensation may be awarded by the court during pendency of the case, which should also be provided in the scheme to be evolved by the Union of India.[8]

Furthermore, the Hon'ble Supreme Court held that the National Commission for Women will have to evolve such scheme as to wipe out the tears of such unfortunate victims. Such a scheme shall be prepared within six months from the date of this judgement. Thereupon, the Union of India, will examine the same and shall take necessary steps for the implementation of the scheme at the earliest.[9]

The recommendations of the National Commission for Women for amending the existing law relating to sexual offences are yet to be undertaken by the Government to change the law which, it is believed, will achieve the objective in reducing the ordeal of the rape victim. The Supreme Court of India, however, has evolved significant principles for the trial of cases of rape and other sexual offences. Underlying the nature of offences, it says that "A rapist not only violates the victims privacy and personal integrity but inevitably causes serious psychological as well as physical harm in the process. Rape is not merely a physical assault - it is often destructive of the whole personality of the victim. A murderer destroys the physical body of his victim, a rapist degrades the very soul of the helpless female.

While laying down significant principles with regard to the appreciation of evidence in such cases, the Hon'ble Court noted that crimes against women in general and rape in particular were on the increase. It noted that "it is an irony that while we are celebrating women's rights in all spheres, we show little or no concern for her honour". It further held that in a matter like rape no self-respecting women would normally come forward to a court of law merely to make a damaging admission against her honour. It stressed that if a court finds it difficult to place implicit reliance on the evidence of the women it may look for evidence which may lend assurance to her testimony. However, to seek coraboration, as is required to be done in the case of an accomplice was not correct in cases of crime against women. The Court also held that the inhibited nature of Indian women and unmarried girls caught in a tradition-bound, non-permissive society are factors that court should not overlook. It noted that how young girls are often reluctant to even admit to any incidents that might sully their family name and honour as they are very conscious of the danger of being ostracised by society. But the fact that the girls do not inform their friends and teachers about the sexual offences committed against them does not detract from their reliability.

The Hon'ble Court asked the trial courts to bear in mind that their observations have a wider implications on society as a whole. It held that even if a victim led a permissive life no reference to the victim as being "a girl of loose moral character" was permissible, for it held that even a promiscusous woman has the right to refuse to submit herself to anyone. It held that there is no justification for rendering such women vulnerable object to satiate man's lust. It is in this context that the Hon'ble Court evolved the rule which is known as the Rape Shield Law in the United States.

This law has come to be accepted as a rule of evidence because of the concern it extend to rape victims. It holds rape to be unique amongst the crimes of all shades and crimes in as much as it permits a total exposure of the private life of its victims. The entire prior sexual history of rape victim is considered permissible as evidence in cross-examination to lend evidence in cross-examination, to lend credence to the fact that the victim has consented to sexual activity in the past. Such rule of admission was justified on the ground that charges of rape are often hurled by vindictive women, and the wild myth that women fantasised being raped. Such evidence was also permitted as it was believed that previous sexual liaisons would undermine the credibility of the woman as a witness. Under the Rape Shield Law, any evidence alluding to the previous sexual history of the victims is considered irrelevant and inadmissible as there is no basis for the assumption that a virgin was more truthful than those who indulged in sexual activity.

Prior sexual activity is thus shut out under the Rape Shield Law, unless the defendant asserts, that the source of semen was someone else's.

In the case of State of Punjab Vs Gurmeet Singh,[10] the Supreme Court has evolved a similar principle by which the prior sexual history of the rape victim can be excluded by trial courts, and the victim can be spared the trauma of having to publicly relive the harrowing experience a second time. This judgement marks a significant step forward and is a rare instance of judge-made law, which brings down the misuse of the provisions of the Evidence Act, taking into account the socio-moral values of the society.

It is hoped that the judgement will slow down if not halt, the slide in the conviction rate of sexual offences. According to the statistics of the National Crime Record Bureau, one rape is committed every 40 minutes, somewhere in the country. Thus, on an average, 37 rapes are committed every day. According to the current rate of conviction, 35 out of the 37 rapists who are arrested, get acquitted or discharged, for one or the other reason, observed the Supreme Court in the Judgment. The adoption of the Rape Shield Law by the Supreme Court, and its understanding and application by the trial courts throughout the length and breadth of the country, holds a ray of hope for rape victims as it invokes a greater sense of fear among rapists.

Matrimonial Offences

Matrimonial offences, though very common, remain unreported as they are performed under strict secrecy. Moreover, the Indian women who is, in all respect, heavily dependent upon her husband is reluctant to seek the judicial redressal. The chapter XX of the Indian Penal Code 1860[11] which contains Sections from 493 to 498 deals with the matrimonial offences. The drafters of the Indian Penal Code observing that the condition of women in India is very different from the west, they are married while still children, they are often neglected for other wives while still young, they share the attention of a husband with several rivals; made special provisions for women. Section 497 of the Indian Penal Code dealing with the offence of adultery reads:

"Whoever has sexual intercourse with a person who is and whom he knows or has reason to believe to be the wife of another man, without the consent or connivance of that man, such sexual intercourse not amounting to the offence of rape, is guilty of the offence of adultery. In such case the wife shall not be punishable as an abettor".[12]

The above Section excludes the women who has equally participated in the crime from being punished even as abettor; only men is liable to be punished under the Section. The constitutionality of this Section was challenged as violative of Articles 14 and 15 of the Indian Constitution but the Hon'ble Supreme Court of India defended this special provision.[13] Despite the fact that matrimonial offences law is designed to protect the women in case of adultery even if the women is an abettor, it is discriminatory against the women as well. The offence of adultery as defined in Section 497 suffers from following defects:

(a) The Section is applicable in those cases where the female partner is the wife of another man. Thus if a man maintains a sexual relationship with an unmarried woman, or concubine, or keep a prostitute, even in the same premises, it is not an offence of adultery. Under the provision of prevention of Immoral Traffic Act, 1956, as amended in 1978 and 1986, a woman is punished by law if she allows several persons to have access to her for sexual intercourse in lieu of consideration of money or in kind. But no such ban has been put on the husband against his extra-marital relations. He has the liberty to choose a sex-partner from amongst unmarried girls, widows or mistresses or he can visit prostitutes. The situation with respect to Muslim women are one of the observing conjungal faithfulness, but the husband can afford to be unfaithful to the wife in sex matters. The Muslim husbands, are enjoying the facility of non-registration of marriages and the benefit of oral 'Talaq' with obligations only to maintain the divorced wife for a period extending to three months only after the oral Talaq.

(b) The husband can, even with the connivance of or the consent of the woman's husband, enjoy sexual pleasure. Thus in each case of prostitution, it can be shown that the woman had a husband and the so-called husband connived or consented to the sexual act, in that event no prosecution can be launched against the person who indulge in this type of sexual activities. This is supported by the fact that somebody else's wife with whom a husband is making love is not punishable under the provision of Section 497 Indian Penal Code the woman not being an abettor. In an act, which amount to a criminal activity with the active connivance of another person involved in the act is neither an abettor nor an accomplice, is against the principal of law.

(c) Under the provision of Section 198 Criminal Procedure Code, 1973 it is the husband who is the aggrieved person in an act of sexual intercourse with his wife. This right is available to the husband of the wife adulterated, whereas, the woman whose husband has been adulterated has no such right to proceed against the woman who had adulterated her husband. This does not make any sense of the right given to a wife vide Section 198(1) (c) Criminal Procedure Code to lodge a complaint against her husband for a bigamous marriage act of her husband.

(d) There are a couple of more problems for such wives. Firstly they have no right under any law of the court so far to a matrimonial home, although there is also no law that she must get out of the husband's home even though the husband is the wrongdoer. This, however is the accepted practice. Secondly under Section 125 Criminal Procedure Code the wife leading a life of adultery is not entitled to maintenance, whereas the wife of the man practising adultery can refuse to live with her husband and yet claim maintenance from him.

Section 497 of the Indian Penal Code is discriminatory in nature as the husband enjoys the right to use the man who had an adulterous sexual act with his wife but the wife has no such right under the law to sue the woman who enticed her husband or with whom her husband had indulged in sexual act.

Prostitution and Trafficking in Women

Prostitution and the trafficking in women has existed and is existing in some form or the other throughout the world. India is no exception. Hundreds of thousands of Indian women are into flesh trade. Quite a number of them are into the trade due to their trafficking into the profession. Moreover, more than one lakh Nepalese women are into flesh trade in India with an additional 5,000 trafficked in every year and thousands more coming from Bangladesh.[14] Despite the laws against prostitution and trafficking in women, the problem continues to perpetuate unabated.

India in pursuance of the International Convention for the Suppression of Immoral Traffic in Women and Girls, 1950 enacted the Suppression of Immoral Traffic in Women and Girls Act, 1956 to suppress the evils of prostitution in women and girls and to provide opportunity to the fallen women and girls to rehabilitate themselves as decent member of the society. The Act did not succeed in ample measure to eradicate or suppress the evils of prostitution and so it was drastically amended in 1978. Besides other stringent measures taken, one progressive measure was the opening of probation under the Probation of Officers Act. However it was soon realised that the measures needed to be more stringent and the provision for release on probation was being abused. So the Parliament again intervened and by Amendment Act, 44 of 1986, completely repealed the provisions relating to probation and provided stricter and higher penalty for offences under the Act. It also realised that time had come when male prostitution should also be covered by the Act, and so it changed the name of the Act from Suppression of Immoral Traffic in Women and Girls to Immoral Traffic (Prevention) Act, 1956.[15] The definition of prostitution has been changed and more gratification of sex without anything more has been taken out of the purview of prostitution. Only where the exploitation or abuse of persons is for commercial purposes, it is prostitution and any places used for such abuse or exploitation is a brothel. A minimum punishment of seven years imprisonment has been prescribed for most of the offences, and this may extend to the years or life imprisonment.

The purpose of the enactment of Immoral Traffic (Prevention) Act, 1956 was to inhibit or to abolish commercialised vice, namely the traffic in women and girls for the purposes of prostitution as an organised means of living. The idea was not to render prostitution per se a criminal offence or punish a women merely because she prostitute herself. A careful scrutiny of the Act reveals that it was aimed at the suppression of the commercialised vice and not at the penalisation of individual prostitute or prostitution itself.

Infact there is no law that directly criminalises prostitution. However, soliciting in a public place is illegal. So is the trafficking in women i.e. engaging in the buying and selling of women for the purpose of prostitution. The law against soliciting obviously makes it impossible for the woman to obtain clients legally. Those women who fall into the lower income brackets obtain clients on the street and public places where they are always being picked up by the police and are vulnerable to all kinds of violence. Usually the sentences are restricted to a fine with a short prison term in addition, for those who have been picked up repeatedly.

There is no law at all against the client, who is definitely an equal participant in the offence. This bias works strongly against the position of the woman. Since the client runs no risk, there is no social motivation to protect the right to livelihood of these women. The women are also then vulnerable to all sorts of pressures from those who traffic in them. The threat of arrest, prison term, police or social violence keeps the women submissive and under control.

There are laws against trafficking in women, with fines and penalties of three to ten years imprisonment as a maximum depending upon whether the woman is a minor girl or not. However it is very difficult to pin the charge on pimps or brothel keepers for several reasons. One is that the woman herself protects them. Also these traffickers have excellent relations with the enforcement personnel and can usually ensure that no charges are preferred against them. Prostitution in India, particularly in the cities and commercial and tourist towns is largely syndicated. In most cases, the brothel owners or pimps stand in court as the legal guardians of the women and the women are returned to their custody in the course of law. Since the current laws permit all the perpetrators, such as client and procurator to get off scot free, while the women who are exploited carry the brunt of social and legal disapproval and penalties. For some women prostitution appears to be the only unfortunate avenue for survival. In order to safeguard the women and the girls we need to evaluate serious measures and implement them in right direction so the biases against the women in current laws may end. Either the prostitution be abolished per se or it should be legalised so that the exploitation of women by pimps, brothel keepers and by the police should end. It is to say, effort to tackle the prostitution must eliminate abuses.

Infanticide and Foeticide

The sex ratio in India has steadily dropped from 992 females per thousand males in 1901 to 929 in 1990. Kerala is the only state where sex-ratio has gone up from 1005 in the year 1901 to 1040 in 1991.[16] In most of other states and union territories the males out number females. The situation is glaring in north-India particularly in the state of Rajasthan. Against the all India figure of 929 females per thousand males the ratio in Rajasthan is 913 females per thousand males. Among the Bhatti Rajputs of the state the sex-ratio is very low, that is 550 females per thousand males. The Thar and Jaisalmer districts of Rajasthan are the areas where the killing of the baby girls is practiced more than other areas.[17] The steadily decline in sex-ratio is due to the combination of several factors like maternity deaths, dowry deaths, malnutrition of both women and girls, crimes such as female infanticide and foeticide etc. The causes for the declining of sex-ratio are more man-made than natural. Infanticide and more so now, foeticide contribute greatly to the low sex-ratio in India.

Infanticide means murder of an infant or a newly born baby. Infanticide as such has not been defined in the Indian Penal Code but since it amounts to the killing of a living person, the sections dealing with murder under the penal code is applicable to the offence of infanticide. Those who kill infants or newly born babies cannot claim the benefit of the right of private defence. Infanticide of the female children in India is usually done out of the undermentioned reasons:

1. Family vanity among the groups of warrior class.
2. Inflated dowry demand by the parents as well as eligible bridegrooms and inability of the bride's parents to meet the same.
3. Heavy expenses is required to be incurred by the bride's party during marriages. The present day practice in a majority of societies is that, in addition to making payments of huge dowry, the bride's parents are required to meet the expenses of both the parties and the groom's parents, at times, shamelessly demand it.
4. At time, craze for a male child drives a family to sacrifice a daughter's life on account of superstitions under the influence of the miracleman of the community.

Foeticide is the unlawful expulsion of foetus. It is also called "criminal abortion" or "causing miscarriage". When used in the legal sense, it includes both abortion and premature labour. As per medical sense, premature labour means expulsion of a child that has attained viability. The term "abortion" or "miscarriage" signify the expulsion of foetus or ovum at an earlier period.[17]

Abortion may be classified into natural and artificial. Natural abortions are common phenomena and may occur due to such reasons as mother's ill-health, local disease, or diseases of the generative organs, shocks, fear, excessive joy, accidental falls etc. Hence, appropriate care is required in respect of the health of the pregnant woman. Premature evacuation of foetus, whether medically, surgically or through indigenous method is known as artificial abortion. Abortion of such nature are becoming common day by day.

In India, termination of pregnancy for reasons other than saving the life of mother (pregnant woman) was a penal offence punishable under Section 312 to 316 of the Indian Penal Code.[19] After India achieved independence and with the passage of time, population started growing rapidly with such an alarming speed that it began to be seen that available resources would not be adequate to meet the necessities of the people in the country. Thus, several family planning programmes were evolved and propagated among the people of the country through mass media. It was further thought that a legislation to legalise termination of pregnancy was another means by which the growing population could be checked. Thus Medical Termination of Pregnancy Act, 1971[20] was enacted as a means of population control. According to it (Section 3), the objective of termination of pregnancy are as follows:

1. **Therapeutic:** When the continuance of pregnancy is likely to endanger the life or the pregnant woman could cause grave injuries to her physical and mental health.
2. **Eugenic**: When there is the risk of the child being born with serious physical or mental handicap. This may occur, if the pregnant woman in the first three months of her pregnancy suffers from (a) German measles; chicken pox or small pox, viral infection including viral hepatitis, toxoplasmonia or any other disease which would have affected the health of the woman; (b) the pregnant woman takes certain medicines, whether under medical advice or otherwise which affect the foetus; (c) the pregnant woman receives radio or any invisible-ray therapy and (d) insanity of the either of the two or both spouse.
3. **Humanitarian:** When the pregnancy is in consequence of sexual assault.
4. **Social:** When the pregnancy has occurred on account of failure of contraceptive device.

Advancement in genetic technology on the other hand provided new techniques, the determination of the abnormalities as well as the sex of the child in advance much before the birth of the child. The pre-natal sex determination is done through aminocentasis, wherein amnetic fluid is drawn through the uterus of a pregnant woman. It is normally possible to determine after sixteen weeks at which stage abortion is risky and can cause injury to the foetus on account of the removal of amnetic fluid. Any defect or physical deformity in the child can, therefore, be attributed on to the parents or the doctor, who drew the fluid. Since the child can not sue either the parents or the doctor, the state is expected to institute legal proceedings against the wrong-doers.

The determination of sex is also possible through Chorionic Villi Sampling (CVS) by vaginal extraction from eight to sixteen weeks of pregnancy. This method is also dangerous as it causes the pregnant woman to infect and in effect spontaneous abortions can take place. It may as well result in fatality of the pregnant woman. The other method of sex determination is through ultra-sound scanning which though non-invasive is unreliable, even at the advanced stage of pregnancy.

The scientists have developed the genetic technology in order to ascertain in advance if the child in the mother's womb has any deformity. However, people in the society are using the know-how to reduce the female population in an organised and systematic manner. The Medical Termination of Pregnancy Act, 1971 only ensures a legal sanction to a Medical Practitioner to abort a female foetus. Thus, the two together, that is Medical Termination of Pregnancy Act, 1971 and sex-determination technology has put India on its way to technological and legal femicide. This created a new problem in bringing a decline in female population.

According to the Provision of Section 3 of the Act, a Registered Medical Practitioner is entitled to abort a foetus within twelve weeks of pregnancy and two of them can abort a pregnancy having a length of 12 to 20 weeks. In either case they will have to take a stand that abortion was necessary in the interest of the health of the woman.

The anguish of a pregnancy by sexual assault is presumed to constitute a grave injury to woman's mental health. However, the failure of a contraceptive device cannot cause any such damage to the mental health. Assessment of the anticipated risk is rather vague and gives a licence to abort female child with the aid of pre-natal sex determination test.

However, business in abortion became possible and flourishing on account of provisions of Section 5 of the Medical Termination of Pregnancy Act, 1971 which is an enabling provision for an emergent situation and permits non-application of provision of Section 3 and Section 4 of the Act. This Section enables a doctor without any experience in gynaecology and obstertics to operate, after having formed an opinion with due care and attention that termination of pregnancy is immediately necessary to save the life of the pregnant woman. It may be pretinent to mention that while making a provision of the Section, care to provide any safeguard has not been introduced to prevent its misuse. A doctor can now be prosecuted under the Indian Penal Code only. The Act suffers from the following flaws:

- (i) The Act does not provide any guidelines for calculating the commencement of pregnancy and to assess the period of twelve weeks or twenty weeks. The matter has been left entirely to the wisdom of the doctor.
- (ii) The Act does not require that pregnant woman counter signature/ or affixes thumb impression on the key column of the register containing details regarding the duration of pregnancy. Thus, any evidence, which, otherwise could have been provided, is always missing.
- (iii) The evidentary value of matter is further weakened by the type of consent Form C prescribed under the Central Rules. There is no column that the doctor makes a declaration that he has explained to the pregnant woman the reason for the termination of her pregnancy.
- (iv) As usual, the Act further ensures a cover for the doctor as per Section 8 of the Act which lays down that, no suit or proceedings shall lie against the doctor if he has acted in good faith. It is very difficult to prove that the doctor did not exercise reasonable care and lacked good faith.

The dangerous form of genetic engineering by selectively aborting the new born child has been flourishing in the capital city of India as well as in several big and small cities of the state on account of no value being attached to a female child in comparison to the male counterpart. In 1983, Bombay had only three sex-clinics and over a period of next five years, it had multiplied to 258 private clinics in addition to the sixteen recognised Government clinics. No permit or licence is required to set up a clinic of this type. On account of the coming up of a large number of clinics, there is a competition in the market and the fees charged (which had become between Rs. 150 to Rs. 500) is within the reach of a common man. The popularity of the method has spread to small places in far-flung areas. The samples now can be carried to Bombay, Delhi, Calcutta or any big city of the country from the nearby places. A survey made by Women's Centre has revealed that out of 8000 abortions checked, 7999 were in respect of females.[21] Consequent upon a widespread resentment against this test, Maharashtra State has taken a lead and the Legislature of Maharashtra Assembly passed the Use of Pre-natal Diagnostic Techniques Act, 1988. The Act, besides prohibiting on unregistered genetic clinic to carry out the pre-natal diagnostic test, lays down the fulfilment of five conditions for the performance of diagnostic tests. The Act if will not achieve the success would atleast exercise the kind of control on the abortion of the female foetus.

Female infanticide and foeticide is an inhuman practice. And what is more ironical is that there is no proper law to tackle the problem. The Government should either ban the pre-natal sex-determination test or if that not be possible, must restrict its general use and confine the use to the recognised institutions. The Medical Termination of Pregnancy Act, 1971 which leaves ample room for the exploitation of prenatal sex determination technology be banned accordingly.

The independent India has enacted a number of legislations to provide as much as possible protection to the women against the various kinds of crimes and atrocities. Most of the pre-independence era, legal provisions have been amended and the existing laws are still being amended from time to time to meet the growing challenges to the life, liberty and dignity of woman. But most of the efforts have either gone futile or have not produced desired results. The rate of crime against women continues to grow at a high rate despite increasing awareness, education and legal safeguards. Not only the centuries old discriminatory practices against women, constitute an important feature of our social life rather they have taken a monstrous form. The kind and nature of crimes against women is taking much brutal and violent form. With every new law, culprits search the loopholes and a safe way to escape. One of the important reason for the rising crime against women in India is the lack of attitudinal change in the society towards women and that of the women as well towards herself.

Most of the incidents of crimes against women go unreported as our society in turn stigmatises the life of the victim specially in cases relating to sexual offences. Besides, laws only grant a legal remedy.

Moreover, most of social legislations to protect women are no more than half-hearted efforts. Social legislation should not only bark but should be able to bite as well. The piece-meal protection provided under different legislations has failed to protect the women.

References

1. *Times of India*, September 19, 1998, p. 4.
2. See for details Appendices-C,C1,C2.
3. *Times of India*, December 19, 1987.
4. See Appendix- D.
5. State of Haryana, Vs Prem Chand and others (1990), *1SCC* 249: 1990 *AIR* (SC) 538.
6. (1995) *1SCC* 14 (19).
7. (1995) *1SCC* 14 (19-20).
8. (1996) *1SCC* 490 (503).
9. (1995) *1SCC* 14 (21).
10. State of Punjab Vs Gurmit Singh and others (1996) *2SCC* 384(403).
11. See for details Appendix-E

13. *AIR* 1954 SC 321; *AIR* 1954 321 (at 322)
14. *Times of India*, August 22, 1998.
15. See for details, Appendices-F, F1.
16. *Hindustan Times*, January 15, 1993.
17. S. Dhaundhial, "Ek Kanya Pujarak Desh Ke Kanya Drohi", *Saptahik Hindustan*, Vol. VII(1), No. 39, 13 to 19 November, 1988, pp. 16-21.
18. Weddel, L. A. Lyons, *Medical Jurisprudence for India*, Thacker Spink & Comp., Calcutta, 1914, p. 288.
19. See *Appendix-G*.
20. See *Appendix-H*.
21. Tripathy, "Child Birth-Paying Head, Ban on Sex-Determination", *India Today*, January 31, 1988, p. 55.

4

Exploitation of Women

A number of crimes are committed against women in India, they are rather on the rise. Moreover there are various other misdeeds and wrongs which are also committed against them but not recognised by the society as something unlawful. Though there are laws to deal with them but normally recourse to law is avoided. The general belief about them is that the law should not be used to settle the private wrongs of the people. The result is that victims suffer silently and do not report their victimization to police or courts. Few of such misdeeds and wrongdoings are discussed here.

Domestic Violence

The problem of domestic violence, the violence in the private realm or violence in the family, is as old as the institution of family itself. This problem is not India specific. It is found in every society though in varying degrees. Though considerable violence occurs in Indian families the problem is not yet recognised as a social problem of disturbing dimensions. Since the people in India eulogize the institution of family, most of them are unwilling to admit its ills. They conveniently tend to ignore or underplay all such factors and forces which produce violence in the confines of family. This is mainly for the reason that family is viewed as a sacred social institution, the bed-rock of Indian society. As such whatever happens in the family is considered as a personal affair and the responsibility of the family members alone not the outsiders. Domestic violence is, therefore, treated more or less as a private affair, an affair to be settled informally and through non-formal measures.

One of the manifestations of domestic violence in the context of women is wife-battering. Wife-battering in both generic and specific sense refers to abuse and victimization of women, generally young wives in comparison of middle and elderly women by their husbands. In fact, wife-battering has been common throughout the ages in different societies and cultures.[1] Unfortunately, it is tolerated and not deemed as an offence untill the wife is subjected to serious assault or cruelty. There appears to be existing a taken for granted cultural norm which makes it legitimate for husbands to beat their wives.

The actual prevalence of wife-battering in Indian society is a matter of conjecture since data are non-existent. Being an invisible phenomenon for most of its parts, it is difficult to figure out how many women get battered at the hands of their husbands. However, it is a matter of common knowledge that it exists amongst all the sections of society; though its occurrence may be higher in lower-income-group-families where women have been traditionally battered because of their illiteracy and dependence on menfolk.[2] It occurs in other sections of the society as well.

Patriarchy is believed to be central cause of wife-battering. Use of physical force has been an integral part of the institution of the family to maintain control in the family. The patriarchal culture is patterned to blame the victim rather than the aggressor. It also legitimises the wife-battering for subordination, domination and control of women. Though there exists unequal power relationship between wife and husband in a patriachal society, it does not necessarily mean that wife abuse is inevitable, it however, does encourage it. The patriarchal society attaches sanctity to the subordination of women, which in turn legitimises their battering as an instrument of keeping them in line. The use of physical force by husbands against their wives is accepted as socially approved instrument of intimidation-an allowable behaviour for a husband. In most societies including Indian wife-battering is commonly perceived as a right of the husband. Besides this, social, cultural, religious and economic factors inter alia exert pressures on the victims not to report the matter to police.

Battered women rarely approach the police for number of reasons: the police being least inclined to intervene in cases of domestic violence; generally side with the husband because most of them being males themselves tend to believe that only wrong women get battered and deservedly so; police generally urge battered women to drop charges or be satisfied with informal warning to the errant husbands. Further, the utilization of police help/protection makes women vulnerable to further assaults. Police sources say that they are hesitant to intervene in cases of domestic violence especially wife-battering because their experience tells them that victims frequently drop charges, withdraw the complaint or simply become unavailable as complaining witnesses. Women complainants of physical abuse, instead of being helped, are advised to go back home which police believe is the right place of grievance redressal. Many policemen nourish the notion that a good wife must not make complaint to any outside person or agency against her husband howsoever bad he may be.[3]

The fact however, is that most battered women silently bear with the situation and do not seek to end their marriages. Obviously these women remain home-bound captives to suffer physical and mental abuse. Silent suffering is their fate because viable alternatives do not exist. Most such women believe that it is their moral duty to preserve and not wreck marriages because marriage is forever for better or worse. A fair number of them do not believe in deserting their husbands who are financially and socially dependent upon their husbands. Many hope that their husbands will change some day. Many have small children and have no resources to raise their children in the absence of father. Some even believe that occasional beating is better than the loneliness and insecurity connected with leaving. Some dread the stigma associated with separation or divorce. Though wife-battering is less common today but it continues to persists. And there seems to be no effective means for controlling the domestic violence-wife-battering other than the overall development of women especially in economic realms.

Sexual Harassment

Sexual harassment like wife-battering is a common instead which is committed against them throughout the world. Sexual harassment is a problem which women face particularly at work-place and educational constitutions. Sexual harassment is generally viewed as unwelcome, sexually determined behaviour (whether directly or by implication) as physical contact and advances; a demand or request for sexual favours; sexually coloured remarks; showing pornography; any other unwelcome physical, verbal or non-verbal conduct of sexual nature.

Though the problem of sexual harassment of women is not new, it has always been in existence. Its recognition, however, as a disturbing social problem is new. Moreover it is rampant every where including India. According to a survey report about the 60 per cent of its respondents who were working women had faced sexual harassment at workplace, 55 per cent of the female students said that they faced such harassment at school or college. Sexual harassment is something faced by most working women. And, however, there seems to be no way out if they approach law and court. Rather they must be ready for some more grave consequences like-loss of job, career prospects and other social problems. Even if the complaint is lodged, women further bear the tedious problems associated with recourse to law with no guarantee that there will be justice at the end. Women who are sexually harassed, therefore, prefer to change the job instead of seeking the help of law. The necessity is to design a law to stop the sexual harassment of women both at work places and institutions of learning or any other place.

The Supreme Court of India prescribed the penalties and prosecution of the person guilty of sexual harassment until a legislation is enacted for the purpose.[4] The Hon'ble Court held that it was the duty of the employer or other responsible person in work places or other institutions, whether public or private, to prevent the commission of acts of sexual harassment and to provide the procedure for the resolution, settlement or prosecution of such acts, which also amounted to misconduct under the relevant disciplinary rules. The guidelines laid down by the Court would be strictly observed in all places, for the preservation and enforcement of the right to gender equality of working women. These directions would be binding and enforceable in law, until suitable legislation is enacted. The guidelines are as follows:

* All employers or persons in charge of work place whether in the public or private sector, should take appropriate steps to prevent sexual harassment. Without prejudice to the generality of this obligation, they should take the following steps.

(a) Express prohibition of sexual harassment which include physical contact and advance, a demand or request for sexual favours, sexually coloured remarks; showing pornography or any other unwelcome physical, verbal or non-verbal conduct of sexual nature; should be noticed, published and circulated in appropriate ways.

(b) The rule or regulation of Government and Public Sector bodies relating to conduct and discipline should include rules prohibiting sexual harassment and provide for appropriate penalties in such rules against the offender.

(c) As regard to private employers, steps should be taken to include the aforesaid prohibitions in the standing order under the Industrial Employment (Standing Orders), Act, 1946.

(d) Appropriate work conditions should be provided in respect of work, leisure, health and hygiene to further ensure that there is no hostile environment towards women at work place and no woman should have reasonable grounds to believe that she is disadvantaged in connection with her employment.

* Where such conduct amounts to specific offences under the Indian Penal Code or under any other law, the employer shall initiate appropriate action in accordance with law by making a complaint with the appropriate authority.

* The victims of sexual harassment should have the option to seek transfer of the perpetrator or their own transfer.

The guidelines prescribed by the Hon'ble Court will serve the purpose of limiting the incidents of sexual harassment.

Widowhood

Widowhood is a curse in Indian society because it subjects to women, especially those who get widowed at young age to inhuman treatment. Widowhood, infact, is the greatest clamity that could befall a Hindu woman who is seen as merging her identity with her husband to be one entity represented by the husband. Social biases and religious injuctions coerce her to live a life of celebacy for the rest of her existence. Describing the pathetic condition of the Hindu widows the proceedings of the Legislative Council of India remarked that "not only must she see no man, she must aviod very approach to ease, finery and pleasure. She must neglect the care of her person, must bear no ornaments, her hair must be shaved or, at least must be worn, dishevelled. She must not see her face in the mirror, nor use perfumes and flowers, must not anoint her body; and her dress must be coarse and dirty".[5] Widowhood reduced the status of women to a dumbdriven cattle.

It is not only the Hindu society which makes a widow distinguishable, the other communities also practice discrimination against a woman in widowhood. Amongst the Muslim widow, marriage is allowed but the widows who get married are given the status of second rate wife. And those who could not get married remain dependent upon relatives and therefore open to exploitation and harassment of different kinds of nature.

Though subjugation of widows is less common today due to the changes in the status of women but they continue to be exploited. Some of the disabilities like non-access to active-participation in auspicious rituals, non-use of any decorations etc continue to be associated with widowhood. In some cases even the head is shaven. Moreover the attitude of the society towards the widowhood remains more or less exploitative having roots in the socio-cultural history of India. A superstitious thinking that exists in the majority of Hindu families is that, widows deserve subjugation on the ground that they are responsible for the untimely demise of their husbands and, therefore, unlucky for the matrimonial home. Despite the fact that Widow Remarriage Act, was passed in 1856 the widow marriages have not yet received the cultural endorsement resulting into its general unacceptability. Unless the cultural and social values change, legislation alone can not stop the subjugation of women in widowhood. Social awareness with economic well-being is essential for the control of exploitation of women in widowhood.

Child Marriage

Women in India are considered a liability right from the time of their birth. They are not seen as individual capable of taking care of themself. They are generally treated as a sort of property, the owner having natural authority to do what he likes with them. As a result girls are married at an early age in both the communities of Hindus and Muslims. The problem of child marriage is primarily rooted in the image of woman as a completely dependent being passing from the custody of her father to that of her husband. Moreover the other socio-economic factors as well, enforce the parents to get off their daughters by marrying them as early as possible.

There is a direct linkage between socio-economic situation and the child-marriage. Poverty and illiteracy are directly related to it. The plight of young girls, belonging to the weaker sections remain pathetic in rural areas. They continue to be treated as unequal, often given away in marriage even before they have learnt the meaning of sex. According to a survey report the lower caste girls are married between the age of five and eleven years. The consent of the girl is never taken. Although these facts relate to eastern part of Uttar Pradesh it is equally applicable[6] to other parts of the country except few like Kerala.

Child-marriage is a serious problem prevalent in whole of India particularly in Rajasthan. A study reveals that there were one hundred lacs girls who were married when they were not even eleven years. A survey of urban population reveals that the majority of the women were married when they were below 18 years of age.[7] A legislation was enacted to stop the child-marriage and thereby their exploitation. The Act, fixed the age of marriage for girls 18 years and for boys 21 years. Despite the law to stop the social menace of child marriage its prevalence continues. Though the picture is not as gloomy as it had been in the past, the socio-economic development has resulted into reduction of number of child-marriages. This menace can only be warded off by eradicating illiteracy and promoting economic well being in general and of women in particular.

Employment

Employment is also an area where the women in India face exploitation. They are paid less wages than their counter-parts for the same kind of work. Indian Constitution guarantees equal pay for equal work for both man and women. In the light of this provision, there should not be any discrimination in the payment of wages on the ground of sex. However the discrimination does exist in the payment of salaries/wages between male and female employees. This discrimination is rampant in unorganised sectors. More than 25 per cent of contract labour comprise of women workers and the uncertainty in their jobs make them highly vulnerable. In many cases they are sacked for refusal to sexual advances of their employers. The low wage and sexual exploitation are symptomatic of a system where even the expression 'contract' is a misnomer, for there is, infact, no contract of any sort, except between the mill/factory management and the labour contractor. This is the area where even male workers are exploited. The situation of women is more vulnerable. They are harassed and exploited considerably in the unorganised sector, especially in construction works, domestic employment, and agriculture sector etc. They are required to work for many hours at meagre wage and either they do not get any holiday or get only a limited number of holidays. Woman in actual practice are at great disadvantageous position in the matter of employment and working conditions.

The National Commission on Self-Employed and Woman in Informal Sector holds that vague labour laws is one of the primary causes for the sorry plight of the women in the country.[8] According to the Commission the basic purpose of these laws gets defeated because they are confined to statue books and are hardly implemented. In case of women workers in unorganised sectors, these difficulties are even more profound. The Rajya Sabha Committee in its report submitted to the House in 1993 observed that "Women workers continue to suffer from inherent inequalities in various sectors of employment and they were often paid less than men notwithstanding the laws. They are kept in conditions almost similar to imprisonment and even subjected to sexual harassment by the contractors." It noted with concern that at several places the women workers were denied full maternity benefits. They were forced to work till advance stages of pregnancy and in some cases their services were terminated when they proceeded on leave. It found more shocking that in private companies women were treated as objects of sex and they were recruited exclusively for selected jobs like those of private secretaries, telephone operators, or receptionists. The Committee felt that in the present social system prevailing in the country a woman is still considered as persona-non-grata. There existed entrenched centres of resistance in society because of which they continue to suffer inequalities. Exploitation of women in employment by even violating the existing laws is a serious problem responsible for lowering the status and dignity of women in the society. Moreover the protective legislation for working women is actually working against them. Employers are reluctant to employ/hire women due to legal safeguards.[9]

The gender difference and bias, places women in India at disadvantageous positions. They are subjected to different kinds of exploitation which make their lives miserably unfortunate. Notwithstanding the Constitution, social and cultural values go against them, thus their exploitation which deprive her of her right to freedom, equality and development. Since the kinds of exploitations discussed here are basically the consequence of social attitude towards women, laws can do little unless the cultural and social values change.

References

1. Martin Del, *Battered Wives*, Glide Publications, San Francisco, 1976; Dobash, R. Emerson and Russel P. Dobash, *Violence Against Wives: A case against Patriarchy;* Free Press, New York, 1979.
2. S.P. Shrivastava, "Domestic Violence: Ramifications and Responses", *Indian Jounal of Crimnology*, Vol. 32(2), pp. 45-63.
3. *Ibid.*
4. *Law Teller*, October 1979.
5. Proceeding of the Legislative Council of India at its meeting on 17 November, 1855, pp. 764-65.
6. Prenav Kumar Chaudhary, *The Sunday Times of India*, January 9, 1994.
7. Editorial Column, "Child marriage", *Hindustan Times*, 18 July, 1988.
8. Ramesh Menon "Contract Workers: Inhuman Bondage", *India Today*, November 30, 1985, pp. 120-123.
9. Iren Tinker, "The Adverse Impact of Development on Women", in Iren Tinker and Michele Bo Bramsen (eds), *Women and World Development*, Overseas Development Council, Washington DC, 1976, pp.22-34.

5

Conclusions

The Constitution of India ensures equality of status to all men and women. It entitles them equal protection of law. It prohibits discrimination as well. Moreover it directs the state to eliminate inequalities in status and opportunities. It provides for the special protection of women. It even provides for the Constitutional guarantee to ensure the enforcement of Fundamental Rights. In fact, it secures as well as protects the basic Human Rights of Indian people.

Despite the Constitutional guarantees and several woman-protective legislations, the ages old pathetic status and position of Indian women largely remains pitable. She suffers gender bias all through her life. It could be in the nature of sex-selective abortions, female foeticide, child-marriage, dowry-deaths, prostitution, sexual violence, sexual harassment, domestic violence, employment discrimination, widow abuse and what not. Though the situation is not so gloomy as it had been in the history. In fifty-years since independence, their status and position has considerably undergone change resulting into their recognisable general welfare. But the fact is that discrimination against them continues. Exploitation is rampant in all walks of life. Crime against them is increasing. The laws, by and large, have proved to be ineffective. They have rather proved to be no more than whitewash. Various reasons are attributable to such an unfortunate plight of women in India.

Though various legislations were enacted to protect the women and to change their status. In fact, they brought some changes in the status of women but largely failed to achieve the stated objectives due to the existing discrepancies in them and their exploitation. Moreover, the nature of the plight and sufferings of women is primarily socio-cultural having roots in history. So there exists a considerable gap between the laws and socio-cultural attitudes, beliefs and traditions which are gender-discriminatory and act as barriers in the proper enforcement of various legislations.

The culture of India is male dominant. It has great bias and discriminatory attitude towards women. The prescriptions of Manu, the socalled great Law-giver, continue to govern the Indian society. His famous dictum that a woman does not deserve freedom so her entire life should be one of dependence on man has bestowed on her a subordinate and inferior status in the society. There are many other such values which either act as a source or catalyst for the crimes against women. So the laws can simply control the exploitation of women having socio-cultural sanctions but can not wipe off the socio-cultural norms which are discriminatory against women. There is need to change such anti-woman attitudes to bridge the gap between them and law, else the laws enacted to ameliorate the status of women will not serve the purpose.

Another significant factor responsible for the plight of women is their poverty, their economic dependence on men. Majority of them remain dependent throughout their lives. First as liability (parayadhan) in the parents house and then in the matrimonial house. Her existence, in reality, is of aquit economic dependence. She is, in fact, discriminated in the matters of inheritance and property both at parents house and matrimonial house. So the change in the economic status of women is essential. This could be done by enacting a legislation providing equal inheritance rights to girls at par with boys and through poverty alleviation programmes.

A co-related factor is the illiteracy of women. A vast majority of them continue to be illiterate and so ignorant. Illiteracy, in fact, prevents them from understanding their rights and from their proper implementation. As illiteracy breads ignorance and helplessness, it should be eradicated through special provisions for promoting female education and other means necessary for the purpose.

The other important causative factor is the complex process of law. The problem is that law exists but women are scared of seeking remedy through law enforcing agencies. Moreover victims generally get no quick redressal. The judicial proceedings are unduely delayed causing great harassment and financial losses to the aggrieved women. The police usually does not move swiftly to secure justice. Neither are the First Information Reports (FIRs) recorded speedily nor any prompt action is initiated unless some pressure is brought on the police. Worst than this is that the conviction is almost negligible. Such a scenario greatly discourages women victims to seek judicial redressal.

Codification of laws is not justice. So no legislation can succeed unless is enforced honestly and sternly. Since this depends both on police and judiciary, there is great need to sensitize both of them towards the problems of women. The biased attitude of police towards women which drives the sanctity from the socio-cultural structure of society needs to be changed. The judiciary should see to it that unnecessary delays in the dispensation of justice are avoided. This change will encourage the women to seek the help of law.

Though it is true that the social problem can not be resolved completely by relying on the instrumentality of law, this does not undermine the importance of law as a vehicle of social change. So, besides removing the discrepancies in the existing legislations, an effort should be made towards the evolution of uniform civil code. It should be so designed that it reduces the exploitations of women under personal laws. Moreover this will be in confirmity with the Constitution of India. This will go a long way in ameliorating the status of women. Devoid of such measures, women in India will continue to be the victims of various kinds of exploitation and subjugation resulting into the increase in the gender specific crimes.

6

Appendices

(A) Universal Declaration of Human Rights

Adopted and proclaimed by General Assembly resolution 217 A (III) of 10 December 1948.

Preamble

Whereas recognition of the inherent dignity of the equal and inalienable rights of all members of the human family is the foundation of freedom, justice and peace in the world,

Whereas disregard and concept for human rights have resulted in barbarous acts which have outraged the conscience of mankind, and the advent of a world in which human beings shall enjoy freedom of speech and belief, and freedom from fear and want has been proclaimed as the highest aspiration of the common people,

Whereas it is essential, if man is not to be compelled to have recourse, as a last resort, to rebellion against tyranny and oppression, that human rights should be protected by the rule of law,

Whereas it is essential to promote the development of friendly relations between nations,

Whereas the people of the United Nations have in the Chapter reaffirmed their faith in fundamental human rights, in the dignity and worth of the human person and in the equal rights of men and women and determined to promote social progress and better standard of life in larger freedom,

Whereas Member States have pledged themselves to achieve, in cooperation with the United Nations, the promotion of universal respect for and observance of human rights and fundamental freedoms,

Whereas a common understanding of these rights and freedom is of the greatest importance for the full realization of this pledge,

now, therefore

The General Assembly,

Proclaims this Universal Declaration of Human Rights as a common standard of achievement for all peoples and all nations, to the end that every individual and every organ of society, keeping this Declaration constantly in mind, shall strive by teaching, and education to promote respect for these rights and freedoms and by progressive measures, national and international, to secure their universal and effective recognition and observance, both among the people of Member States themselves and among the people of territories under their jurisdiction.

Article 1

All human beings are born free and equal in dignity and rights. They are endowed with reason and conscience and should act towards one another in a spirit of brotherhood.

Article 2

Everyone is entitled to all rights and freedoms set forth in this Declaration, without distinction of any kind, such as race, colour, sex, language, religion, political or other opinion, national or social origin, property, birth or other status.

Furthermore, no distinction shall be made on the basis of the political jurisdiction or international status of the country or territory to which a person belongs, whether it be independent, trust, non-self-governing or under any other limitation of sovereignty.

Article 3

Everyone has the right to life, liberty and security of person.

Article 4

No one shall be held in slavery or servitude; slavery and the slave trade shall be prohibited in all their forms.

Article 5

No one shall be subjected to torture or to cruel, inhuman or degrading treatment or punishment.

Article 6

Everyone has the right to recognition everywhere as a person before the law.

Article 7

All are equal before the law and are entitled without any discrimination to equal protection of the law. All are entitled to equal protection against any discrimination in violation of this Declaration and against any incitement to such discrimination.

Article 8

Everyone has the right to an effective remedy by the competent national tribunals for acts violating the fundamental rights granted him by the constitution or by law.

Article 9

No one shall be subjected to arbitrary arrest, detention or exile.

Article 10

Everyone is entitled in full equality to a fair and public hearing by an independent and impartial tribunal, in the determination of his rights and obligations and of any criminal charge against him.

Article 11

1. Everyone charged with a penal offence has the right to be presumed innocent, until proved guilty according to law in a public trial at which he had all the guarantees necessary for his defence.
2. No one shall be held guilty of any penal offence on account of any act or omission which did not constitute a penal office, under national or international law, at

the time when it was committed. Nor shall a heavier penalty be imposed than the one that was applicable at the time the penal offence was committed.

Article 12

No one shall be subjected to arbitrary interference with his privacy, family home or correspondence, nor to attacks upon his honour and reputation. Everyone has right to the protection of the law against such interference or attacks.

Article 13

1. Everyone has the right to freedom of movement and residence within the borders of each State.
2. Everyone has the right to leave any country, including his own, and to return to his country.

Article 14

1. Everyone has the right to seek and to enjoy in other countries asylum from persecution.
2. This right may not be invoked in the case of prosecutions genuinely arising from non-political crimes or from acts country to the purpose and principles of the United Nations.

Article 15

1. Everyone has the right to a nationality.
2. No one shall be arbitrary deprived of his nationality nor denied the right to change his nationality.

Article 16

1. Men and women of full age, without any limitation due to race, nationality or religion, have the right to marry and to found a family. They are entitled to equal rights as to marriage, during marriage and at its dissolution.
2. Marriage shall be entered into only with the free and full consent of the intending spouses.
3. The family is the natural and fundamental group unit of society and is entitled to protection by society and the State.

Article 17

1. Everyone has the right to own property alone as well as in association with others.
2. No one shall be arbitrarily deprived of his property.

Article 18

Everyone has the right to freedom of thought, conscience and religion; this right includes freedom to change his religion or belief, and freedom, either alone or in community with others and in public or private, to manifest his religion or belief in teaching, practice, worship and observance.

Article 19

Everyone has the right to freedom of opinion and expression; this right includes freedom to hold opinions without interference and to seek, receive and impart information and ideas through any media and regardless of frontiers.

Article 20

1. Everyone has the right to freedom of peaceful assembly and association.
2. No one may be compelled to belong to an association.

Article 21

1. Everyone has the right to take part in the government of his country, directly or through freely chosen representatives.
2. Everyone has the right to equal access to public service in his country.
3. The will of the people shall be the basis of the authority of government; this will shall be expressed in periodic and genuine elections which shall be by universal and equal suffrage and shall be held by secret vote or by equivalent free voting procedures.

Article 22

Everyone, as a member of society, has the right to social security and is entitled to realization, through national effort and international co-operation and in accordance with the organization and resources of each States, of the economic, social and cultural rights indispensable for his dignity and the free development of his personality.

Article 23

1. Everyone has the right to work, to free choice of employment, to just conditions of work and to protection against unemployment.
2. Everyone, without any discrimination has the right to equal pay for equal work.
3. Everyone who has the right to just and favourable remuneration ensuring for himself and his family an existence worthy of human dignity, and supplemented, if necessary by other means of social protection.
4. Everyone has the right to form and to join trade unions for the protection of his interests.

Article 24

Everyone has the right to rest and leisure, including reasonable limitation of working hours and periodic holidays with pay.

Article 25

1. Everyone has the right to a standard of living adequate for the health and well-being of himself and of his family, including food, clothing, housing and medical care and necessary social services, and the right to security in the event of unemployment, sickness, disability, widowhood, old age or other lack of livelihood in circumstances beyond his control.
2. Motherhood and childhood are entitled to special care and assistance. All children, whether born in or out of wedlock, shall enjoy the same social protection.

Article 26

1. Everyone has the right to education. Education shall be free, at least in the elementary and fundamental stages. Elementary education shall be compulsory. Technical and professional education shall be made generally available and higher education shall be equally accessible to all on the basis of merit.

2. Education shall be directed to the full development of the human personality and to the strengthening of respect for human rights and fundamental freedoms. It shall promote understanding, tolerance and friendship among all nations, racial or religious groups, and shall further the activities of the United Nations for the maintenance of peace.
3. Parents have a prior right to choose the kind of education that shall be given to their children.

Article 27

1. Everyone has the right freely to participate in the cultural life of the community, to enjoy the arts and to share in scientific advancement and its benefits.
2. Everyone has the right to the protection if the moral and material interests resulting from any scientific, literacy or artistic production of which he is the author.

Article 28

Everyone is entitled to a social and international order in which the rights and freedoms set forth in this Declaration can be fully realized.

Article 29

1. Everyone has duties to the community in which alone the free and full development of his personality is possible.
2. In the exercise of his rights and freedoms, everyone shall be subject only to such limitations as are determined by law solely for the purpose of securing due recognition and respect for the rights and freedoms of other and of meeting the just requirements of morality, public order and the general welfare in a democratic society.
3. These rights and freedoms may in no case be exercised contrary to the purpose and principles of the United Nations.

Article 30

Nothing in this Declaration may be interpreted as implying for any State, group of person any right to engage in any activity or to perform any act aimed at the destruction of any of the rights and freedoms set forth herein.

(B) Women's Rights: Convention on the Elimination of all forms of Discrimination against Women, 1979

Adopted by General Assembly resolution 34/180 of 18 December, 1979.

Preamble

The States Parties to the present Convention,

Noting that the Charter of the United Nations reaffirms faith in fundamental human rights, in the dignity and worth of the human person and in the equal rights of men and women,

Noting that the Universal Declaration of Human Rights affirms the principle of the inadmissibility of discrimination, and proclaims that all human beings are born free and equal in dignity and rights and that everyone is entitled to all the rights and freedoms set forth therein, without distinction of any kind, including distinction based on sex,

Noting that the States Parties to the International Covenants on Human Rights have the obligation to ensure the equal right of men and women to enjoy all economic, social, cultural, civil and political rights,

Considering the international conventions concluded under the auspices of the United Nations and the specialized agencies promoting equality of rights of men and women,

Noting also the resolutions, declarations and recommendations adopted by the United Nations and the specialized agencies promoting equality of rights of men and women,

Concerned, however, that despite these various instruments extensive discrimination against women continues to exist,

Recalling that discrimination against women violates the principles of equality of rights and respect for human dignity, is an obstacle to the participation of women, on equal terms with men, in the political, social, economic and cultural life of their countries, hampers the growth of the prosperity of society and the family and makes more difficult the full development of the potentialities of women in the service of their countries and of humanity,

Concerned that in situation of poverty women have the least access to food, health, education, training and opportunities for employment and other needs,

Convinced that the establishment of the new international economic order based on equality and justice will contribute significantly towards the promotion of equality between men and women,

Emphasizing that the eradication of *apartheid*, all forms of racism, racial discrimination. colonialism, neo-colonialism, aggression, foreign occupation and domination and interference in the internal affairs of States is essential to the full enjoyment of the rights of men and women.

Affirming that the strengthening of international peace and security, the relaxation of international tension, mutual co-operation among all States irrespective of their social and economic systems, general and complete disarmament, in particular nuclear disarmament under strict and effective international control, the affirmation of the principles of justice, equality and mutual benefit in relations among countries and the realization of the right of people under alien and colonial domination and foreign occupation to self-determination and independence, as well as respect for national sovereignty and territorial integrity, will promote social progress and development and as consequence will contribute to the attainment of full equality between men and women,

Convinced that the full and complete development of a country, the welfare of the world and the cause of peace require the maximum participation of women on equal terms with men in all field,

Bearing in mind the great contribution of women to the welfare of the family and to the development of society, so far not fully recognized, the social significance of maternity and the role of both parents in the family and in the upbringing of children, aware that the role of women in procreation should not be a basis for discrimination but that the upbringing of children requires a sharing of responsibility between men and women and society as a whole,

Aware that a change in the traditional role of men as well as the role of women in society and in the family is needed to achieve full equality between men and women,

Determined to implement the principles set forth in the Declaration on the Elimination of Discrimination against Women and, for that purpose, to adopt the measures required for the elimination of such discrimination in all its forms and manifestations, have agreed on the following:

Article 1

For the purposes of the present Convention, the term "discrimination against women" shall mean any distinction, exclusion or restriction made on the basis of sex which has the effect or purpose of impairing or nullifying the recognition, enjoyment or exercise by women, irrespective of their marital status, on a basis of equality of men and women, of human rights and fundamental freedoms in the political, economic, social,cultural, civil or any other field.

Article 2

States Parties condemn discrimination against women in all its form, agree to pursue by all appropriate means and without delay a policy of eliminating discrimination against women and, to this end, undertake:

(a) to embody the principle of the equality of men and women in their national constitutions or other appropriate legislation if not yet incorporated therein and to ensure, through law and other appropriate means, the practical realization of this principle;

(b) To adopt appropriate legislative and other measures, including sanctions where appropriate, prohibiting all discrimination against women;

(c) To establish legal protection of the rights of women of an equal basis with men and to ensure through component national tribunals and other public institutions the effective protection of women against any act of discrimination;

(d) To refrain from engaging in any act or practise of discrimination against women and to ensure that public authorities and institution shall act in conformity with this obligation;

(e) To take all appropriate measures to eliminate discrimination against women by any person, organization or enterprise;

(f) To take all appropriate measures, including legisation, to modify or abolish existing laws, regulations, customs and practices which constitute discrimination against women;

(g) to repeal all national penal provisions which constitute discrimination against women.

Article 3

States parties shall take in all fields, in particular in the political, social, economic and cultural fields, all appropriate measures, including legislation, to ensure the full development and advancement of women, for the purpose of guaranteeing them the exercise and enjoyment of human rights and fundamental freedoms on a basis of equality with men.

Article 4

1. Adoption by States Parties of temporary special measures aimed at accelerating *de facto* equality between men and women, shall not be considered discrimination as defined in the present Convention, but shall in no way entail as a consequence the maintenance of unequal or separate objectives of equality of opportunity and treatment have been achieved.

2. Adoption by States Parties of special measures, including those measures contained in the present Convention, aimed at protecting maternity shall not be considered discriminatory.

Article 5

States Parties shall take all appropriate measures:

(a) To modify the social and cultural patterns of conduct of men and women, with a view to achieving the elimination of pejudices and customary and all other practices which are based on the idea of the inferiority or the superiority of either of the sexes or on stereotyped roles for men and women;

(b) To ensure that family education includes a proper understanding of maternity as a social function, and the recognition of the common responsibility of men and women in the upbringing and development of their children, it being understood that the interest of the children is the primordial consideration in all cases.

Article 6

States Parties shall take all appropriate measures, including legislation, to suppress all forms of traffic in women and exploitation of prostitution of women.

Article 7

States Parties shall take all appropriate measures to eliminate discrimination against women in the political and public life of the country and, in particular, shall ensure to women, on equal terms with men, the right:

(a) To vote in all elections and public referenda and to be eligible for election to all publicly elected bodies;

(b) To participate in the formulation of government policy and the implementation thereof and to hold public office and perform all public functions at all levels of government:

(c) To participate in non-governmental organizations and associations concerned with the public and political life of the country.

Article 8

States Parties shall take all appropriate measures to ensure to women, on equal terms with men and without any discrimination, the opportunity to represent their

Governments at the international level and to participate in the work of international organizations.

Article 9

1. States Parties shall grant women equal rights with men to acquire, change or retain their nationality. They shall ensure in particular that neither marriage to an alien nor change of nationality by the husband during marriage shall automatically change the nationality of the wife, render her stateless or force upon her the nationality of the husband.
2. States Parties shall grant women equal rights with men with respect to the nationality of their children.

Article 10

States Parties shall take all appropriate measures to eliminate discrimination against women in order to ensure to them equal rights with men in the field of education and in particular to ensure, on a basis of equality of men and women:

(a) The same conditions for career and vocational guidance, for access to studies and for the achievement of diplomas in educational establishments of all categories in rural as well as in urban areas; this equality shall be ensured in pre-school, general, technical, professional and higher technical education, as well as in all types of vocational training;

(b) Access to the same curricula, the same examination, teaching staff with qualifications of the same standard and school premises and equipment of the same quality,

(c) The elimination of any stereotyped concept of the roles of men and women at all levels and in all forms of education by encouraging coeducation and other types of education which will help to achieve this aim and, in particular, by the revision of textbooks and school programmes and the adaption of teaching methods;

(d) The same opportunities to benefit from scholarships and other study grants;

(e) The same opportunities for access to programmes of continuing education, including adult and functional literacy programmes, particularly those aimed at reducing, at the earliest possible time, any gap in education existing between men and women;

(f) The reduction of female student drop-out rates and the organization of programmes for girls and women who have left school prematurely;

(g) The same opportunities to participate actively in sports and physical education;

(h) Access to specific educational information to help to ensure the health and well being of families, including information and advice on family planning.

Article 11

1. States Parties shall take all appropriate measures to eliminate discrimination against women in the field of employment in order to ensure, on a basis of equality of men and women, the same rights in particular:

    (a) The right to work as an inalienable right of all human beings;

    (b) The right to the same employment opportunities, including the application of the same criteria for selection in matters of employment;

    (c) The right to free choice of profession and employment, the right to promotion, job security and all benefits and conditions of service and the right to receive vocational training and retraining, including apprenticeships advance vocational training and recurrent training;

    (d) The right to equal remuneration, including benefits and to equal treatment in respect of work of equal value as well as equality of treatment in the evaluation of the quality of work;

    (e) The right to social security, particularly in cases of retirement, unemployment, sickness, invalidity and old age and other incapacity to work, as well as the right to paid leave;

    (f) The right to protection of health and to safety in working conditions, including the safeguarding of the function of the reproduction.

2. In order to prevent discrimination against women on the grounds of marriage or maternity and to ensure their effective right to work, States Parties shall take appropriate measures:
   (a) To prohibit, subject to the imposition of sanctions, dismissal on the grounds of pregnancy or of maternity leave and discrimination in dismissals on the basis of martial status;
   (b) To introduce maternity leave with pay or with comparable social benefits without loss of former employment, seniority or social allowances;
   (c) To encourage the provision of the necessary supporting social services to enable parents to combine family obligations with work responsibilities and participation in public life, in particular through promoting the establishment an development of a network of child-care facilities;
   (d) To provide special protection to women during pregnancy in types of work proved to be harmful to them.
3. Protective legislation relating to matters covered in this article shall be reviewed periodically in the light of scientific and technological knowledge and shall be revised, repealed or extended as necessary.

Article 12

1. States Parties shall take all appropriate measures to eliminate discrimination against women in the field of health care in order to ensure, on a basis of equality of man and women access to health care services, including those related to family planning.
2. Notwithstanding the provisions of paragraph of this article, States Parties shall ensure to women appropriate services in connection with pregnancy, confinement and the post-natal period, granting free services where necessary, as well as adequate nutrition during pregnancy and lactation.

Article 13

States Parties shall take all appropriate measures to eliminate discrimination against women in other areas of economic and social life in order to ensure, on a basis of equality of men and women, the same rights, in particular;

(a) The right to family benefits;

(b) The right to bank loans, mortgages and other forms of financial credit;

(c) The right to participate in recreational activities, sports and all aspects of cultural life.

Article 14

1. States Parties shall take into account the particular problems faced by rural women and the significant roles which rural women play in the economic survival of their families including their work in the non-monetized sectors of the economy, and shall take all appropriate measures to ensure the application of the provisions of the present Convention to women in rural areas.
2. States Parties shall take all appropriate measures to eliminate discrimination against women in rural areas in order to ensure, on a basis of equality of men and women, that they participate in and benefit from rural development and, in particular, shall ensure to such women the right:

   (a) To participate in elaboration and implementation of development planning at all levels;

   (b) To have access to adequate health care facilities, including information, counselling and services in family planning;

   (c) To benefit directly from social security programmes;

   (d) To obtain all types of training and education, formal and non-formal, including that relating to functional literacy, as well as, *inter alia*, the benefit of all community and extension services, in order to increase their technical proficiency;

   (e) To organize self-help groups and co-operatives in order to obtain equal access to economic opportunities through employment or self-employment;

(f) To participate in all community activities;

(g) To have access to agricultural credit and loans, marketing facilities, appropriate technology and equal treatment in land and agrarian reform as well as in land resettlement schemes;

(h) To enjoy adequate living conditions, particularly in relation to housing, sanitation, electricity and water supply, transport and communications.

Article 15

1. States Parties shall accord to women equality with men before the law.
2. States Parties shall accord to women, in civil matters, a legal capacity identical to that of men and the same opportunities to exercise that capacity. In particular, they shall give women equal rights to conclude contracts and to administer property and shall treat them equally in all stages of procedure in courts and tribunals.
3. States Parties agree that all contracts and all other private instruments of any kind with a legal effect which is directed at restricting the legal capacity of women shall be deemed null and void.
4. States Parties shall accord to men and women the same rights with regard to the law relating to the movement of persons and the freedom to choose their residence and domicile.

Article 16

1. States Parties shall take all appropriate measures to eliminate discrimination against women in all matters relating to marriage and family relations and in particular shall ensure, on a basis of equality of men and women:

(a) The same right to enter into marriage;

(b) The same right freely to choose a spouse and to enter into marriage only with their free and full consent;

(c) The same rights and responsibilities during marriage and at its dissolution;

(d) The same rights and responsibilities as parents, irrespective of their marital status, in matters relating to their children; in all cases the interest of the children shall be paramount;

(e) The same rights to decide freely and responsibly on the number and spacing of their children and to have access to the information, education and means to enable them to exercise these rights;

(f) The same rights and responsibilities with regard to guardianship, wardship, trusteeship and adoption of children, or similar institutions where these concepts exists in national legislation; in all cases the interest of the children shall be paramount:

(g) The same personal rights as husband and wife, including the right to choose a family name, a profession and an occupation;

(h) The same rights for both spouses in respect of the ownership, acquisition, management, administration, enjoyment and disposition of property, whether free of charge or for a valuable consideration.

2. The betrothal and the marriage of a child shall have no legal effect, and all necessary action, including legislation, shall be taken to specify a minimum age for marriage and to make the registration of marriages in an official registry compulsory.

Article 17

1. For the purpose of considering the progress made in the implementation of the present Convention, there shall be established a Committee on the Elimination of Discrimination against Women (hereinafter referred to as the Committee) consisting, at the time of entry into force of the Convention, of eighteen and after ratification of or accession to the Convention by the thirty fifth State Party, of twenty-three experts of high moral standing and competence in the field covered by the Convention. The experts shall be elected by States Parties from among their nationals and shall

serve in their personal capacity, consideration being given to equitable geographical distribution and to the respresentation of the different forms of civilization as well as the principal legal systems.

2. The members of the Committee shall be elected by secret ballot from a list of persons nominated by States Parties. Each State Party may nominate one person from among its own nationals.

3. The initial election shall be held six months after the entry into force of the present Convention. At least three months before the date of each election of the Secretary-General of the United Nations shall address a letter to the States Parties inviting them to submit their nominations within two months. The Secretary-General shall prepare a list in alphabetical order of all persons thus nominated, indicating the States Parties which have nominated them, and shall submit it to the States Parties.

4. Elections of the members of the Committee shall be held at a meeting of States Parties convened by the Secretary-General at United Nations Headquarters. At that meeting, for which two thirds of the States Parties shall constitute a quorum, the persons elected to the committee shall be those nominees who obtain the largest number of votes and an absolute majority of the votes of the representatives of States Parties present and voting.

5. The member of the Committee shall be elected for a term of four years. However, the terms of nine of the members elected at the first election shall expire at the end of two years: immediately after the first election the names of these nine members shall be chosen by lot by the Chairman of the Committee.

6. The election of the five additional members of the Committee shall be held in accordance with the provisions of paragraphs, 3 and 4 of this article, following the thirty-fifth ratification or accession. The terms of two of the additional members elected on this occasion shall expire at the end of two years, the names

of these two member having been chosen by lot by the Chairman of the Committee.

7. The members of the Committee shall, with the approval of the General Assembly, receive emoluments from United Nations resources on such terms and conditions as the Assembly may decide, having regard to the importance of the Committee's responsibilities.
8. The Secretary-General of the United Nations shall provide the necessary staff and facilities for the effective performance of the function of the Committee under the present Convention.

Article 18

1. States Parties undertake to submit to the Secretary-General of the United Nations, for consideration by the Committee, a report on the legislative, judicial, administrative or other measures which they have adopted to give effect to the provisions of the present Convention and on the progress made in this respect:
   (a) Within one year after the entry into force for the State concerned;
   (b) Thereafter at least every four years and further whenever the Committee so requests.
2. Reports may indicate factors and difficulties affecting the degree of fulfilment of obligations under the present Convention.

Article 19

1. The Committee shall adopt its own rules of procedure.
2. The Committee shall elect its officers for a term of two years.

Article 20

1. The Committee shall normally meet for a period of not more than two weeks annually in order to consider the reports submitted in accordance with article 8 of the present Convention.
2. The meetings of the Committee shall normally be held at United Nations Headquarters or at any other convenient place as determined by the Committee.

Article 21

1. The Committee shall, through the Economic and Social Council, report annually to the General Assembly of the United Nations on its activities and may make suggestions and general recommendations based on the examination of reports and information received from the States Parties. Such suggestions and general recommendations shall be included in the report of the Committee together with comments, if any, from States Parties.
2. The Secretary-General of the United Nations shall transmit the reports of the Committee to the Commission on the Status of Women for its information.

Article 22

The specialized agencies shall be entitled to be represented at the consideration of the implementation of such provisions of the present Convention as fall within the scope of their activities. The Committee may invite the specialized agencies to submit reports on the implementation of the convention in areas falling within the scope of their activities.

Article 23

Nothing in the present Convention shall affect any provisions that are more conducive to the achievement of equality between men and women which may be contained;

(a) In the legislation of a State Party; or

(b) In any other international convention, treaty or agreement in force for that State.

Article 24

States Parties undertake to adopt all necessary measures at the national level aimed at achieving the full realization of the rights recognized in the present Convention.

Article 25

1. The present Convention shall be open for signature by all States.
2. The Secretary-General of the United Nations is designated as the depositary of the present Convention.

3. The present Convention is subject to ratification. Instruments of ratification shall be deposited with the Secretary-General of the United Nations.
4. The present Convention shall be open to accession by all States. Accession shall be effected by the deposit of an instrument of accession with the Secretary-General of the United Nations.

Article 26

1. A request for the revision of present Convention may be made at any time by any State Party by means of a notification in writing addressed of the Secretary-General of the United Nations.
2. The General Assembly of the United Nations shall decide upon the steps, if any, to be take in respect of such a request.

Article 27

1. The present Convention shall enter into force on the thirtieth day after the date of deposit with the Secretary-General of the United Nations of the Twentieth instrument of ratification or accession.
2. For each State ratifying the present Convention or acceding to it after the deposit of twentieth instrument of ratification or accession, the Convention shall enter into force on the thirtieth day after the date of the deposit of its own instrument of ratification or accession.

Article 28

1. The Secretary-General of the United Nations shall receive and circulate to all States the text of reservations made by States at the time of ratification or accession.
2. A reservation incompatible with the object and purpose of the present Convention shall not be permitted.
3. Reservations may be withdrawn at any time by notification to this effect addressed to the Secretary-General of the United Nations, who shall then inform all States thereof. Such notification shall take effect on the date on which it is received.

Article 29

1. Any dispute between two or more States Parties concerning the interpretation or application of the present Convention which is not settled by negotiation shall, at the request of one of them, be submitted to arbitration. If within six months from the date of the request for arbitration the parties are unable to agree on the organization of the arbitration, any one of those parties may refer the dispute to the International Court of Justice by request in conformity with the Statute of the Court.
2. Each State Party may at the time of signature or ratification of the present Convention or accession be there to declare that it does not consider itself bound by paragraph of this article. The other States Parties shall not be bound by that paragraph with respect to any State Party which has made such a reservation.
3. Any State Party which has made a reservation in accordance with paragraph of this article may at any time withdraw that reservation by notification to the Secretary-General of the United Nations.

Article 30

The present Convention, the Arabic, Chinese, English, French, Russian and Spanish texts of which are equally authentic, shall be deposited with the Secretary-General of the United Nations.

In witness whereof the undersigned, duly authorized, have signed the present Convention.

(C) The Dowry Prohibition Act, 1961

An Act to prohibit the giving or taking of dowry.

Be it enacted by Parliament in the Twelfth Year of the Republic of India as follows:

Short title extent, and commencement

(1) This Act may be called the Dowry Prohibition Act, 1961.

(2) It extends to the whole of India except the State of Jammu and Kashmir.

(3) It shall come into force on such date as the Central Government may by notification in the Official Gazette, appoint.

Definition of "Dowry"

In this Act, "dowry" means any property or valuable security given or agreed to be given either directly or indirectly-

(a) by one party to a marriage to the other party to the marriage, or

(b) by the parents of either party to a marriage or by any other person, to either party to the marriage or to any other person;

at or before or after the marriage as consideration for the marriage of the said parties, but does not include dower or mahr in the case of persons to whom the Muslim Personal Law (*Shariat*) applies.

Explanation-I: For the removal of doubts, it is hereby declared that any presents made at the time of a marriage to either party to the marriage in the form of cash, ornaments, clothes or other articles, shall not be deemed to be dowry within the meaning of this section, unless they are made as consideration for the marriage of the said parties.

Explanation-II: The expression "valuable security" has the same meaning as in Section 30 of the Indian Penal Code (45 of 1860).

Penalty for giving or taking dowry

If any person after the commencement of this Act, gives or takes or abets the giving or taking of dowry, he shall be punishable with imprisonment which may extend to six months, or with fine which may extend to five thousand rupees, or with both.

Penalty for demanding dowry

If any person, after the commencement of this Act, demands, directly or indirectly, from the parents or guardian of a bride or bridegroom, as the case may be, any dowry, he shall be punishable with imprisonment which may extend to six months, or with fine which may extend to five thousand rupees, or with both:

Provided that no court shall take cognizance of any offence under this section except with the previous sanction of the State Government or of such officer as the State Government may, by general or special order, specify in this behalf.

Agreement for giving or taking dowry to be void

Any agreement for the giving or taking of dowry shall be void.

Dowry to be for the benefit of the wife or her heirs

(1) Where any dowry is received by any person other than the woman in connection with whose marriage it is given, that person shall transfer it to the woman-

(a) if the dowry was received before marriage, within one year after the date of marriage; or

(b) if dowry was received at the time of or after the marriage, within one year after the date of its receipt; or

(c) if the dowry was received when the woman was a minor within one year after she has attained the age of eighteen years; and pending such transfer, shall hold it in trust for the benefit of the woman.

(2) If any person fails to transfer any property as required by subsection (1) and within the time limited therefor, he shall be punishable with imprisonment which may extend to six months, or with fine which may exend to five thousand rupees, or with both; but such punishment shall not absolve the person from his obligation to transfer the property as required by sub-section (1).

(3) Where the woman entitled to any property under sub-section (1) dies before receiving it, the heirs of the woman shall be entitled to claim it from the person holding it for the time being.

(4) Nothing contained in this section shall affect the provisions of section 3 or section 4.

Cognizance of Offences

Notwithstanding anything contained in the Code of Criminal Procedure, 1898 (5 of 1898)-

(a) no court inferior to that of a Presidency Magistrate or a Magistrate of the First Class shall try any offence under this Act;

(b) no court shall take cognizance of any such offence except on a complaint made within one year from the date of the offence:

(c) it shall be lawful for a Presidency Magistrate or a Magistrate of the First Class to pass any sentence authorised by this Act on any person convicted of an offence under this Act.

Offences to be non-cognizable, bailable and non-compoundable

Every offence under this Act shall be non-cognizable, bailable and non-compoundable.

Power to make rules

(1) The Central Government may, by notification in the Official Gazette, make rules for carrying out the purposes of this Act.

(2) Every rule made under this section shall be laid as soon as may be after it is made before each House of Parliament while it is in session for a total period of thirty days which may be comprised in one session or in two successive sessions, and if before the expiry of the session in which it is so laid or the session immediately following, both Houses agree in making any modification in the rule or both Houses agree that the rule should not be made, the rule shall therefore have effect only in such modified form or be of no effect, as the case may be, so however that any such

modified form or be of no effect, as the case may be, so however that any such modification on annulment shall be without prejudice to the validity of anything previously done under that rule.

The Andhra Pradesh Dowry Prohibition Act, 1958 (Andhra Pradesh Act 1 of 1958) and the Bihar Dowry Restraint Act, 1950 (Bihar Act 25 of 1950), are hereby repealed.

(C-1) The Dowry Prohibition (Maintenance of Lists of Presents to the Bride and Bridegroom) Rules, 1985

Notification

G.S.R. 664(E) - In exercise of the powers conferred by section 9 of the Dowry Prohibition Act, 1961 (28 of 1961), the Central Government hereby make the following rules, namely :

Short Title and Commencement

(1) These rules may be called the Dowry Prohibition (Maintenance of Lists of Presents to the Bride and Bridegroom) Rules, 1985.

(2) They shall come into force on the 2nd day of October, 1985 being the date appointed for the coming into force of the Dowry Prohibition (Amendment) Act, 1984 (63 of 1984).

Rules in accordance with lists of presents are to be maintained

(1) The lists of presents which are given at the time of marriage to the bride shall be maintained by the bride.

(2) The lists of presents which are given at the time of marriage to the bridegroom shall be maintained by the bridegroom.

(3) Every list of presents referred to in sub-rule (1) or sub-rule (2) -

(a) shall be prepared at the time of the marriage or as soon as possible after the marriage;

(b) shall be in writing;

(c) shall contain;

(i) a brief description of each present;

(ii) the approximate value of the present;

(iii) the name of the person who has given the present; and,

(iv) where the person giving the present is related to the bride or bridegroom, a description of such relationship;

(d) shall be signed by both the bride and the bridegroom.

Explanation-1: Where the bride is unable to sign, she may affix her thumb-impression in lieu of the signature after having the list read out to her and obtaining the signature, on the list, of the person who has so read out the particulars contained in the list.

Explanation-2: Where the bridegroom is unable to sign, he may affix his thumb-impression in lieu of his signature after having the list read out to him and obtaining the signature on the list, of the person who has so read out the particulars contained in the list.

(4) The bride or the bridegroom may, if she or he so desires, obtain on either or both of the lists referred to in sub-rule (1) or sub-rule (2) the signature or signatures of any relations of the bride or the bridegroom or of any other person or persons present at the time of the marriage.

(C.2) The Dowry Prohibition (Amendment) Act, 1986

An Act, further to amend the Dowry Prohibition Act, 1961, and to make certain necessary changes in the Indian Penal Code, the Code of Criminal Procedure, 1973 and the Indian Evidence Act, 1872.

Be it enacted by Parliament in the Thirty-Seventh Year of the Republic of India as follows:

Short Title and Commencement

(1) This Act may be called the Dowry Prohibition (Amendment) Act, 1986.

(2) It shall come into force on such date as the Central Government may, by notification in the Official Gazette, appoint.

Amendment of Section 2

In the Dowry Prohibition Act, 1961 (28 of 1961) (hereinafter referred to as the principal Act), in section 2, for the words "or after the marriage", the words "or any time after the marriage" shall be substituted.

Amendment of Section 3

(a) In the opening paragraph, for the words "six months, but which may extend to two years, and with fine which may extend to ten thousand rupees or the amount of the value of such dowry, whichever is more", the words "five years, and with fine which shall not be less than fifteen thousand rupees or the amount of the value of such dowry, whichever is more" shall be substituted;

(b) in the provison, for the words "six months", the words "five years" shall be substituted.

Insertion of new Section 4A

After section 4 of the principal Act, the following section shall be inserted, namely:

Ban on Advertisement

If any person-periodical, journal or through any other media, any share in:

(a) offers, through any advertisement in any newspaper, his property or of any money or both as a share in any business or other interest as consideration for the marriage of his son or daughter or any other relative,

(b) prints or publishes or circulates any advertisement referred to in clause (a).

He shall be punishable with imprisonment for a term which shall not be less than six months, but which may extend to five years, or with fine which may extend to fifteen thousand rupees:

Provided that the Court may, for adequate and special reasons to be recorded in the judgement, impose a sentence of imprisonment for a term of less than six months."

Amendment of Section 6

In Section 6 of the principal Act,—

(a) in sub-section (2),—

(i) after the words "time limit specified therefore", the words, brackets and figure "or as required by sub-section (3)," shall be inserted;

(ii) for the words "which may extend to ten thousand rupees", the words "which shall not be less than five thousand rupees, but which may extend to ten thousand rupees" shall be substituted;

(b) in sub-section (3) the following proviso shall be inserted, namely:

"Provided that where such woman dies within seven years of her marriage, otherwise than due to natural causes, such property shall—

(a) if she has no children, be transferred to her parents, or

(b) if she has children, be transferred to 'such children and pending such transfer, be held in trust for such children,";

(c) in sub-section (3A),—

(i) after the word, brackets and figure "sub-section (1)" the words, brackets and figure "or sub-section (3)" shall be inserted;

(ii) for the words "her heirs", wherever they occur, the words "her heirs, parents or children" shall be substituted.

Amendment of Section 7

In Section 7 of the principal Act, after sub-section (2), the following sub section shall be inserted, namely:

"(3) Notwithstanding anything contained in any law for the time being in force, a statement made by the person aggrieved by the offence shall not subject such person to a prosecution under this Act."

Amendment of Section 8

In Section 8 of the principal Act, in sub-section (2) for the word "bailable", the word "non-bailable" shall be substituted.

Insertion of new Section 8A and 8B

After Section 8 of the principal Act, the following sections shall be inserted, namely:

"Burden of proof in certain cases"

8A. Where any person is prosecuted for taking or abetting the taking of any dowry under Section 3, or the demanding of dowry under Section 4, the burden of proving that he had not committed an offence under those sections shall be on him.

Dowry Prohibition Officers

8B. (1) The State Government may appoint as many Dowry Prohibition Officers as it thinks fit and specify the areas in respect of which they shall exercise their jurisdiction and powers under this Act.

(2) Every Dowry Prohibition Officer shall exercise and perform the following powers and functions, namely:

(a) to see that the provisions of this Act are complied with;

(b) to prevent, as far as possible, the taking or abetting the taking of, or the demanding of, dowry;

(c) to collect such evidence as may be necessary for the prosecution of persons committing offences under the Act; and

(d) to perform such additional functions as may be assigned to him by the State Government, or as may be specified in the rules made under this Act.

(3) The State Government may, by notification in the Official Gazette, confer such powers of a police officer as may be specified in the notification on the Dowry Prohibition Officer who shall exercise such powers subject to such limitations and conditions as may be specified by rules made under this Act.

(4) The State Government may, for the purpose of advising and assisting the Dowry Prohibition Officers in the efficient performance of their functions under this Act, appoint an advisory board consisting of not more than five social welfare workers (out of whom at least two shall be women) from the area in respect of which such Dowry Prohibition Officer exercises jurisdiction under sub-section(1)".

Substitution of new section for Section 10

For section 10 of the principal Act, the following section shall be substituted, namely:

Power of the State Government to make rules

(1) The State Government may, by notification in the Official Gazette, make rules for carrying out the purposes of this Act.

(2) In particular, and without prejudice to the generality of the foregoing power, such rules may provide for all or any of following matters, namely:

(a) the additional functions to be performed by the Dowry Prohibition Officers under sub-section (2) of Section 8B.

(b) limitations and conditions subject to which a Dowry Prohibition Officer may exercise his functions under sub-section (3) of Section 8B.

(3) Every rule made by the State Government under this section shall be laid as soon as may be after it is made before the State Legislature."

Amendment of Act, 45 of 1860

In the Indian Penal Code after Section 304A, the following section shall be inserted, namely:

Dowry Death

304B. (1) Where the death of a woman is caused by any burns or bodily injury or occurs otherwise than under normal circumstances within seven years of her marriage and it is shown that soon before her death she was subjected to cruelty of harassment by her husband or any relative of her husband for, or in connection with, any demand for dowry, such death shall be called "dowry death", and such husband or relative shall be deemed to have caused her death.

Explanation: For the purpose of this sub-section, "dowry" shall have the same meaning as in Section 2 of the Dowry Prohibition Act, 1961 (28 of 1961).

(2) Whoever commits dowry death shall be punished with imprisonment for a term which shall not be less than seven years but which may extend to imprisonment for life."

Amendment of Act 2 of 1974

In the Code of Criminal Procedure, 1973, in the First Schedule after the entries relating to Section 304A, the following entries shall be inserted, namely:

Section	*Offence*	*Punishment*	*Cognizable or non Cognizable*	*Bailable non-bailable*	*By what Court triable*
1	*2*	*3*	*4*	*5*	*6*
"304B	*Dowry death*	*Imprisonment of not less than seven years but which may extend to imprisonment for life.*	*Ditto*	*Non-bailable*	*Court of session"*

Amendment of Act 1 of 1872

In the Indian Evidence Act, 1872, after Section 113A, the following section shall be inserted, namely:

"Presumption as to dowry death

113B. When the question is whether a person has committed the dowry death of a woman and it is shown that soon before her death such woman had been subjected by such person to cruelty or harassment for, or in connection with, any demand for dowry, the Court shall presume that such person had caused the dowry death.

Explanation: For the purposes of this section, "dowry death" shall have the same meaning as in Section 304B of the Indian Penal Code (45 of 1860)"

(D) Sexual Offences: Indian Penal Code, Sections 375 to 376

Section 375

Rape

A man is said to commit "rape" who except in the case hereinafter excepted, has sexual intercourse with a woman under circumstances falling under any of the six following descriptions:-

First - Against her will.

Secondly - Without her consent.

Thirdly - With her consent, when her consent has been obtained by putting her or any person in whom she is interested in fear of death or hurt.

Fourthly - With her consent, when the man knows that he is not her husband, and that her consent is given because she believes that he is another man to whom she is or believes herself to be lawfully married.

Fifthly - With her consent, when, at the time of giving such consent, by reason of unsoundness of mind or intoxication or the administration by him personally or through another of any stupefying or unwholesome substance, she is unable to understand the nature and consequences of that to which she gives consent.

Sixthly - With or without her consent, when she is under sixteen years of age.

Explanation: Penetration is sufficient to constitute the sexual intercourse necessary to the offence of rape.

Exception: Sexual intercourse by a man with his own wife, the wife not being under fifteen years of age, is not rape.

Section 376

Punishment for rape

(1) Whoever, except in the cases provided for by sub section-2, commits rape shall be punished with imprisonment of either description for a term which shall not be less than seven years, but which may be for life or for a term which may extend to ten years and shall also be liable to fine unles the woman raped is his own wife and is not under twelve years of age, in which case, he shall be punished with imprisonment of either description for a term which may extend to two years or with fine or with both:

Provided that the court may, for adequate and special reasons to be mentioned in the judgement, impose a sentence of imprisonment for a term of less than seven years.

(2) Whoever-

(a) being a police officer commits rape-

(i) within the limits of the police station to which he is appointed; or

(ii) in the premises of any station house whether or not situated in the police station to which he is appointed; or

(iii) on a woman in his custody or in the custody of a police officer subordinate to him; or

(b) being a public servant, takes advantage of his official position and commits rape on a woman in his custody as such public servant or in the custody or a public servant subordinate to him; or

(c) being on the management or on the staff of a jail, remand home or other place of custody established by or under any law for the time being in force or of a woman's or children's institution takes advantage of his official position and commits rape on any inmate of such jail, remand home, place or institution; or

(d) being on the management or on the staff of a hospital, takes advantage of his official position and commits rape on a woman in that hospital; or

(e) commits rape on a woman knowing her to be pregnant; or

(f) commits rape on a woman when she is under twelve years of age; or

(g) commits gang rape,

shall be punished with rigorous imprisonment for a term which shall not be less than ten years but which may be for life and shall also be liable to fine:

Provided that the court may, for adequate and special reasons to be mentioned in the judgement, impose a sentence of imprisonment of either description for a term of less than ten years.

Explanation 1: Where a woman is raped by one or more in a group of persons acting in furtherance of their common intention, each of the persons shall be deemed to have committed gang rape within the meaning of this sub-section.

Explanation 2: "Woman's, or children's institution" means an institution whether called an orphanage or a home for neglected woman or children or a widow's home or by any other name, which is established and maintained for the reception and care of woman or children.

Explanation 3: "Hospital" means the precincts and includes the precincts of any institution for the reception and treatment of persons during convalescence or of persons requiring medical attention or rehabilitation.

376-A. Intercourse by a man with his wife during separation. Whoever has sexual intercourse with his own wife, who is living separately from him under a decree of separation or under any custom or usage without her consent shall be punished with imprisonment of either description for a term which may extend to two years and shall also be liable to fine.

376-B. Intercourse by public servant with woman in his custody- whoever, being a public servant, takes advantage of his official position and induce or seduces, any woman, who is in his custody as such public servant or in the custody of a public servant subordinate to him, to sexual intercourse with him, such sexual intercourse not amounting to the offence of rape, shall be punished with imprisonment of either description for a term which may extend to five years and shall also be liable to fine.

376-C. Intercourse by superintendent of Jail, remand home, etc. - whoever, being the superintendent or manager of a Jail, remand home or other place or custody established by or under any law for the time being in force or of a woman's or children's institution takes advantage of his official position and induces or seduces any female inmate of such jail, remand home, place or institution to have sexual intercourse with him, such sexual intercourse not amounting to the offence of rape, shall be punished with imprisonment of either description for a term which may extend to five years and shall also be liable to fine.

Explanation-1: "Superintendent" in relation to a jail, remand home or other place of custody or a women's or children's institution includes a person holding any other office in such jail, remand home, place or institution by virtue of which he can exercise any authority or control over its inmates.

Explanation 2: The expression "women's or children's institution " shall have the same meaning as in explanation to sub-section (2) of Section 376.

376-D. Intercourse by any member of the management or staff of hospital with any woman in that hospital- Whoever being on the management of a hospital or being on the staff of a hospital takes advantage of his position and has sexual intercourse with any woman in that hospital, such sexual intercourse not amounting to the offence of rape, shall be punished with imprisonment of either description for a term which may extend to five years and shall also be liable to fine.

Explanation 3: The expression "hospital" shall have the same meaning as in Explanation 3 sub-section (2) of Section 376.

(1) Amendment of Section 327- In the Code of Criminal Procedure, 1973 (hereinafter referred as the Criminal Procedure Code), Section 327 shall be renumbered as sub-section (i) of that section and after it, as so renumbered, the following sub-sections shall be inserted, namely—

(2) Notwithstanding anything contained in sub-section (1) the inquiry into and trial of rape or an offence under Section 376, Section 376 A. Section 376 B, Section 376 C or Section 376 D of the Indian Penal Code shall be conducted in camera:

Provided that the presiding Judge may, if he thinks fit, or on an application made by either of the parties, allow any particular person to have access to, or be or remain in, the room or building used by the court.

(3) Where any proceedings are held under sub-section (2), it shall not be lawful for any person to print or publish any matter in relation to any proceedings, except with the previous permission of the court.

Amendment of the First Schedule - In the First Schedule to the Criminal Procedure Code, under the heading "1-Offences under the Indian Penal Code"-

(a) after the entries relating to Section 228, the following entries shall be inserted, namely :-

1	2	3	4	5	6
228A	Disclosure of identity of the victim of certain offences, etc.	Imprisonment for two years and fine	Cognizable	Bailable	Any Magistrate
	Printing or publication of a proceeding without prior permission of court.	Ditto	Ditto	Ditto	Ditto

Further restrictions are placed with regard to the publication of Court proceedings under Section-2 the above Criminal Law Amendment preventing the disclosure of the identity of the victims thus:

Disclosure of identity of the victim of certain offences, etc.- In the Indian Penal Code (hereinafter referred to as the Penal Code), after Section 228, the following section shall be inserted, namely:

228 A.(1) Whoever prints or publishes the name or any matter which may make known the identity of any person against whom an offence under Section 376, Section 376 A. Section 376B, Section 376C or Section 376D is alleged or found to have been committed (hereinafter in this section referred to as the victim) shall be punished with imprisonment of either description for a term which may extend to two years and shall also be liable to fine.

(2) Nothing in sub-section (1) extend to any printing or publication of the name or any matter which may make known the identity of the victim if such printing or publication is-

(a) by or under the order in writing of the officer-in-charge of the police station of the police officer making the investigation into such offence action in good faith for the purposes of such investigation; or

(b) by, or with the authorisation in writing of the victim; or

(c) where the victim is dead or minor or of unsound mind, by, or with the authorisation in writing or, the next of kin of the victim.

Provided that no such authorisation shall be given by the next of kin to anybody other than the chairman or the secretary, by whatever name called, of any recognised welfare institution or organisation.

Explanation: For the purposes of this sub-section, "recognised welfare institution or organisation" means a social welfare institution or organisation recognised in this behalf by the Central or State Government.

(3) Whoever prints or publishes any matter in relation to any proceeding before a court with respect to an offence referred to in sub-section (1) without the previous permission of such court shall be punished with imprisonment of either description for a term which may extend to two years and shall also be liable to fine.

Explanation: The printing or publication of the judgement of any High Court or the Supreme Court does not amount to an offence within the meaning of this section.

(E) Matrimonial Offences, Indian Penal Code, Sections 493 to 498

Section 493: Cohabitation caused by a man deceitfully inducing a belief of lawful marriage

Every man who by deceit, causes any woman who is not lawfully married to him to believe that she is lawfully married to him and to cohabit or have sexual intercourse with him in that belief, shall be punished with imprisonment of either description for a term which may extend to ten years and shall be liable to fine.

Section 494: Marrying again during lifetime of husband or wife

Whoever, having a husband or wife living, marries in any case, in which such marriage is void by reason of its taking place during the life of such husband or wife, shall be punished with imprisonment of either description for a term which may extend to seven years, and shall also be liable to fine.

Exception

This section does not extend to anyperson whose marriage with such husband or wife has been declared void by a Court of competent jurisdiction, nor to any person who contracts a marriage during the life of a former husband or wife, if such husband or wife, at the time of the subsequent marriage, shall have been continually absent from such person for the space of seven years, and shall have been heard of by such person as being alive within that time provided the person contracting such subsequent marriage shall, before such marriage takes place, inform the person with whom such marriage is contracted of the real state of acts so far as the same are within his or her knowledge.

Section 495: Same offence with concealment of former marriage from person with whom subsequent marriage is contracted

Whoever commits the offence defined in the last preceding section having concealed from the person with whom the subsequent marriage is contracted, the fact of the former marriage, shall be punished with imprisonment of either description for a term which may extend to ten years, and shall also be liable to fine.

Section 496: Marriage ceremony fraudulently gone through without lawful marriage

Whoever, dishonestly or with a fraudulent intention, goes through the ceremony of being married, knowing that he is not there by lawfully married, shall be punished with imprisonment of either description for a term which may extend to seven years, and shall also be liable to fine.

Section 497: Adultery

Whoever has sexual intercourse with a person who is and whom he knows or has reason to believe to be the wife of another man, without the consent or connivance of that man, such sexual intercourse not amounting to the offence of rape, is guilty, of the offence of adultery, and shall be punished with imprisonment of either description for a term which may extend to five years, or with fine, or with both. In such case the wife shall not be punishable as an abettor.

Section 498: Enticing or taking away or detaining with criminal intent a married woman

Whoever takes or entices away any woman who is and whom he knows or has reason to believe to be the wife of any other man, from that man, or from any person having the care of her on behalf of that man, with intent that she may have illicit intercourse with any person, or conceals or detains with that intent any such woman, shall be punished with imprisonment of either description for a term which may extend two years or with fine, or with both.

(F) The Suppression of Immoral Traffic in Women and Girls Act, 1956

An Act to provide in pursuance of the International Convention signed at New York on the 9th day of May, 1950, for the suppression of immoral traffic in women and girls.

Be it enacted by Parliament in the Seventh Year of the Republic of India as follows :

Short extent and commencement

1. This Act may be called The Suppression of Immoral Traffic in Women and Girls Act, 1956.
2. It extends to the whole of India.
3. This section shall come into force at once; and the remaining provision of this Act shall come into force on such date as the Central Government may, by notification in the Official Gazette, appoint.

Definitions

In this Act, unless the context otherwise requires,

(a) "brothel" includes any house, room, or place or any portion of any house, room or place, which is used for purposes of prostitution for the gain of another person or for the mutual gain of two or more prostitutes;

(b) "girl" means a female who has not completed the age of twenty-one years;

(c) "magistrate" means a District Magistrate, a Sub. Divisional Magistrate a Presidency Magistrate, or a Magistrate of the first class specially empowered by the State Government, by notification in the Official Gazette exercise jurisdiction under this Act;

(d) "prescribed" means prescribed by rules made under this Act;

(e) "prostitute" means a female who offers her body for promiscuous sexual intercourse for hire, whether in money or in kind;

(f) "Prostitution" means the act of a female offering her body for promiscuous sexual intercourse for hire, whether in money or in kind;

(g) "protective home" means an institution, by whatever name called, in which women and girls may be kept in pursuance of this Act and includes-

(i) a shelter where female under-trials may be kept in pursuance of this Act; and

(ii) a corrective institution in which women and girls rescued and detained under this Act may be imparted such training and instruction and subjected to such disciplinary to their reformation and the prevention of offences under this Act;

(h) "public place" means any place intended for use by or accessible to the public and includes any public conveyance;

(i) "special police officer" means a police officer appointed by or on behalf of the State Government to be in charge of police duties within a specified area for the purpose of this Act;

(j) "women " means a female who has completed the age of twenty-one years.

Punishment for keeping a brothel or allowing premises to be used as a brothel

(1) Any person who keeps or manages, or acts or assists in the keeping or management of a brothel shall be punishable on first conviction with rigorous imprisonment for a term of not less than one year and not more than three years and also with fine which may extend to two thousand rupees and in the event of a second or subsequent conviction, with rigorous imprisonment for a term of not less than two years and not more than five years and also with fine which may extend to two thousand rupees.

(2) Any person who

(a) being the tenant, lessee, occupier or person in charge of any premises, uses, or knowingly allows any other person to use, such premises or any part thereof as a brothel or

(b) being the owner, lessor or landlord of any premises or the agent of such owner, lessor or landlord, lets the same or any part thereof with the knowledge that the same or any part thereof is intended to be used as a brothel, or is wilfully a party to the use of such premises or any part thereof as a brothel,

shall be punishable on first conviction with imprisonment for a term which may extend to two years; and with fine which may extend to two thousand rupees and in the event of a second or subsequent conviction, with rigorous imprisonment for a term which may extend to five years and also with fine.

(3) Notwithstanding anything contained in any other law for the time being in force,on conviction of any person referred to in clause (a) or clause (b) or sub-section (2) of any offence under that sub-section in respect of any premises or any part thereof, any lease or agreement under which such premises have been leased out or are held or occupied at the time of the commission of the offence, shall become void and

inoperative with effect from the date of the said conviction.

Punishment for living on the earnings of prostitution

(1) Any person over the age of eighteen years who knowingly lives, wholly or in part, on the earnings of the prostitution of a woman or girl shall be punishable with imprisonment for a term which may extend to two years, or with fine which may extend to one thousand rupees, or with both.

(2) Where any person is proved-

(a) to be living with, or to be habitually in the company of a prostitute; or

(b) to have exercised control, direction or influence over the movements of a prostitute in such a manner as to show that such person is aiding, abetting or compelling her prostitution; or

(c) to be acting as a tout or pimp on behalf of a prostitute,

it shall be presumed, until the contrary is proved, that such person is knowingly living on the earnings of prostitution of another person within the meaning of sub-section (1) :

provided that no such presumption shall be drawn in the case of son or daughter of a prostitute, if the son or daughter is below the age of eighteen years.

Procuring, inducing or taking woman or girl for the sake of prostitution

(1) Any person who -

(a) procures or attempts to procure a woman or girl, whether with or without her consent, for the purpose of prostitution ; or

(b) induces a woman or girl to go from any place with the intent that she may for the purpose of prostitution become the inmate of, or frequent, a brothel ; or

(c) takes or attempts to take a woman or girl, or causes a woman or girl to be taken, from one place to another with a view to her carrying on, or being brought up to carry on prostitution ; or

(d) causes or induces a woman or girl to carry on prostitution;

shall be punishable on first conviction with rigorous imprisonment for a term of not less than one year and not more than two years and also with fine which may extend to two thousand rupees.

(2) In the event of a second or subsequent conviction of an offence under this section a person shall be punishable with rigorous imprisonment for a term of not less than two years and not more than five years and also with fine which may extend to two thousand rupees.

(3) An offence under this section shall be triable -

(a) in the place from which a woman or girl is procured, induced to go, taken or caused to be taken or from which an attempt to procure or take such woman or girl is made; or

(b) in the place to which she may have gone as a result of the inducement or to which she is taken or caused to be taken or an attempt to take her is made.

Detaining a woman or girl in premises where prostitution is carried on

(1) Any person who detains any woman or girl, whether with or without her consent,

(a) in any brothel, or

(b) in or upon any premises with intent that she may have sexual intercourse with any man other than her lawful husband,

shall be punishable on first conviction with rigorous imprisonment for a term of not less than one year and not more than two years and also with fine which may extend to two thousand rupees.

(2) On a second or subsequent conviction for an offence under this section a person shall be punishable with rigorous imprisonment for a term of not less than two years and not more than five years and also with fine which may extend to two thousand rupees.

(3) A person shall be presumed to detain a woman or girl in a brothel or in or upon any premises for the purposes of sexual intercourse with a man other than her lawful husband, if such person, with intent to compel or induce her to remain there-

(a) withholds from her any jewellery, wearing apparel, money or other property belonging to her, or

(b) threatens her with legal proceedings if she takes away with her any jewellery, wearing apparel, money or other property lent or supplied to her by the direction of such person.

(4) Notwithstanding any law to the contrary, no suit, prosecution or other legal proceeding shall lie against such woman or girl at the instance of the person by whom she has been detained, for the recovery of any jewellery, wearing apparel or other property alleged to have been lent or supplied to or for such woman or girl or to have been pledged by such woman or girl or for the recovery of any money alleged to be payable by such woman or girl.

Prostitution in or in the vicinity of public places

(1) Any woman or girl who carries on prostitution, and the person with whom such prostitution is carried on, in any premises which are within a distance of two hundred yards of any place of public, religious worship, educational institution, hostel, hospital, nursing home or such other public place of any kind as may be notified in this behalf by the Commissioner of Police or District Magistrate in the manner prescribed, shall be punishable with imprisonment for a term which may extend to three months.

(2) Any person who

(a) being the keeper of any public place knowingly permits prostitutes for purposes of their trade to resort to or remain in such place; or

(b) being the tenant, lessee, occupier or person in charge of any premises referred to in sub-section (1) knowingly permits the same or any part thereof to be used for prostitution; or

(c) being the owner, lessor or landlord of any premises referred to in sub-section (1), or the agent of such owner, lessor or landlord, lets the same or any part thereof with the knowledge that the same or any part thereof may be used for prostitution, is or is wilfully a party to such use;

shall be punishable on first conviction with imprisonment for a term which may extend to three months, or with fine which may extend to two hundred rupees, or with both, and in the event of a second or subsequent conviction with imprisonment for a term which may extend to six months and also with fine which may extend to two hundred rupees.

Seducing or soliciting for purpose of prostitution

Whoever, in any public place or within sight of and in such manner as to be seen or heard from any public place, whether from within any building or house or not-

(a) by words, gestures, wilful exposure of her person (whether by sitting by a window or on the balcony of a building or house or in any other way), or otherwise tempts or endeavours to tempt, or attracts or endeavours to attract the attention of, any person for the purpose of prostitution; or

(b) solicits or molests any person, or loiters or acts in such manner as to cause obstruction; or annoyance to persons residing nearby or passing by such public place or to offend against public decency, for the purpose of prostitution,

shall be punishable on first conviction with imprisonment for a term which may extend to six months, or with fine which may extend to five hundred rupees, or with both and in the event of second or subsequent conviction, with imprisonment for a term which may extend to one year, and also with fine which may extend to five hundred rupees.

Seduction of a woman or girl in custody

(1) Any person who having the custody, charge of care of any woman or girl cause or aids or abets the seduction for prostitution of that woman or girl shall be punishable on first conviction with rigorous imprisonment for a term of not less than one year and not more than three years, and also with fine which may extend to one thousand rupees.

(2) In the event of a second or subsequent conviction of an offence under this section a person shall be punishable with imprisonment which may extend to five years and also with fine which may extend to one thousand rupees.

Probation of good conduct and detention in protective home

(1) (a) A person convicted for the first time of any offence under sub-section (2) of section 3, or under section 4, section 5, section 7 or section 8 may having regard to his age, character, antecedents and the circumstances in which the offence was committed be released by the Court before which he is convicted on probation of good conduct in the manner provided in sub-section (1) of section 562 of the Code of Criminal Procedure, 1898.

(b) A person convicted for the first time of any offence under section 7 or section 8 may, having regard to his age, character, antecedents and the circumstances in which the offence was committed, also be released with admonition in the manner provided for in sub-section (1A) of section 562 of the Code of Criminal Procedure, 1898.

(c) The provision of sub-section (2), sub-section (3) and sub-section (4) of section 562 and section 563 and section 564 of the Code of Criminal Procedure, 1898, shall apply to cases referred to in clause (a) and clause (b).

(2) Where a woman or girl is convicted of any offence under section 7 or section 8 and is not released under clause (a) of sub-section (1) on probation of good conduct or under clause (b) of that sub-section with admonition, the Court convicting the woman or girl may, having regard to the age, character, antecedents of the woman or girl and the circumstances in which the offence was committed pass in lieu of the sentence of imprisonment or fine, a sentence of detention in a protective home for a period of not less than two years and not more than five years.

(3) Notwithstanding anything contained in the Code of Criminal Procedure, 1898, or any other law for the time being in force, no person convicted under sub-section (1) of section 3 or under section 6 or section 9 shall be released on probation or with admonition

Notification of address of previously convicted offenders

(1) When any person having been convicted-

(a) by a Court in India of an offence punishable under this Act or punishable under section 363, section 365, section 366, section 366A, section 366B,section 367, section 368, section 370, section 371, section 371, section 372 or section 373 of the Indian Penal Code, with imprisonment for a term of two years or upwards; or

(b) by a Court or Tribunal in any other country of an offence which would, if committed in India, have been punishable under this Act or under any of the aforesaid sections with imprisonment for a like term,

is within a period of five years after release from prison, again convicted of any offence punishable under this Act or under any of those section with imprisonment for a term of two years or upwards by a Court, such Court may, if it thinks fit at the time of passing the sentence of imprisonment on such person, also order that his residence, and any change of or absence from, such residence, after release be notified according to rules made under section 23 for a period not exceeding five years from the date of expiration of that sentence.

(2) If such conviction is set aside on appeal or otherwise, such order shall become void.

(3) An order under this section may also be made by an Appellate Court or by the High Court when exercising its powers of revision.

(4) Any person charged with a breach of any rule referred to in sub-section (1) may be tried by a Magistrate of competent jurisdiction in the district in which the place last notified as his residence is situated.

Security for good behaviour from habitual offenders

(1) When a Court convicting a person of an offence under this Act finds that he has been habitually committing or attempting to committing, or attempting to commit, or abetting the commission of, that offence or any other offence under this Act and the Court is of opinion that it is necessary or desirable to require that person to execute a bond for good behaviour, such Court may at the time of passing the sentence on the person order him to execute a bond for a sum proportionate to his means with or without sureties for his good behaviour during such period not exceeding three years as it thinks fit.

(2) If the conviction is set aside on appeal or otherwise the bond so executed shall become void.

(3) An order under this section may also be made by an Appellate Court or by the High Court when exercising its powers of revision.

(4) When a Magistrate receives information from the police or otherwise that any person within the local limits

of his jurisdiction habitually commits, or attempts to commit, or abets the commission of, any offence under this Act, such Magistrate may require such person to show cause why he should not be ordered to execute a bond with sureties for his good behaviour for such period not exceeding three years as the Magistrate thinks fit and thereupon the provisions of sections 112 to 126 of the Code of Criminal Procedure, 1898, shall apply in such a case.

Special police officer and advisory body

(1) There shall be for each area to be specified by the State Government in this behalf a special police officer appointed by or on behalf of that Government for dealing with offences under this Act in that area.

(2) The special police officer shall not be below the rank of—

(a) an Assistant Commissioner of Police in the presidency towns of Madras and Calcutta;

(b) a Superintendent of Police in the presidency town of Bombay; and

(c) a Deputy Superintendent of Police elesewhere.

(3) For the efficient discharge of his functions in relation to offences under this Act-

(a) the special police officer of an area shall be assisted by such number of subordinate police officers (including women police officers wherever practicable) as the State Government may think fit; and

(b) the State Government may associate with the special police officer a non-official advisory body consisting of not more than five leading social welfare workers of that area (including women social welfare workers wherever practicable) to advise him on questions of general importance regarding the working of this Act.

Offences to be cognizable

Notwithstanding anything contained in the Code of Criminal Procedure, 1898, any offences punishable under this Act shall be deemed to be cognizable offence within the meaning of that Code:

provided that, notwithstanding anything contained in that Code—

(i) arrest without warrant may be made only by the special police officer or under his direction or guidance, or subject to his prior approval;

(ii) when the special police officer requires any officer subordinate to him to arrest without warrant otherwise than in his presence any person for an offence under this Act, he shall give that subordinate officer an order in writing, specifying the person to be arrested and the offence for which the arrest is being made; and the latter officer before arresting the person shall inform him of the substance of the order and, on being required by such person, show him order;

(iii) any police officer not below the rank of Inspector specially authorised by the special police officer may, if has reason to believe that on account of delay involved in obtaining the order of the special police officer,and valuable evidence relating to any offence under this Act is likely to be destroyed or concealed or the person who has committed or is suspected to have committed the offence is likely to escape or if the name and address of such a person is unknown or there is reason to suspect that a false name or address has been given, arrest the person concerned without such order, but in such a case he shall report, as soon as may be, to the special police officer the arrest and the circumstances in which the arrest was made.

Search without warrant

(1) Notwithstanding anything contained in any other law for the time being in force, whenever the special police

officer has reasonable grounds for believing that an offence punishable under this Act has been or is being committed in respect of a women or girl living in any premises, and that search of the premises with warrant cannot be made without undue delay, such officer may, after recording the grounds of his belief, enter and search such premises without a warrant.

(2) Before making a search under sub-section (1), the special police officer shall call upon two or more respectable inhabitants (at least one of whom shall be a women) of the locality in which the place to be searched is situated, to attend and witness the search, and may issue an order in writing to them or any of them so to do.

(3) Any person who, without reasonable cause, refuses or neglects to attend and witness a search under this section, when called upon to do so by an order in writing delivered or tendered to him shall be deemed to have committed an offence under section 187 of the Indian Penal Code.

(4) The special police officer entering any premises under sub-section (1) shall be entitled to remove therefrom any girl, if in his opinion she is under the age of twenty-one years and is carrying on or is being made to carry on, or attempts are made to make her carry on prostitution.

(5) The special police officer, after removing the girl under sub-section (4) shall forthwith produce her before the appropriate Magistrate.

(6) The special police officer and other persons taking part in, or attending and witnessing a search shall not be liable to any civil or criminal proceedings against them in respect of anything lawfully done in connection with or for the purpose of the search.

Rescue of girl

(1) Where a Magistrate has reason to believe, from information received from the police or otherwise, that

a girl apparently under the age of twenty-one years, is living, or is carrying on, or is being made to carry on prostitution, in a brothel, he may direct the special police officer to enter such brothel, and to remove therefrom such girl and produce her before him.

(2) The special police officer after removing the girl shall forthwith produce her before the Magistrate issuing the order.

Intermediate custody of girls removed under section 15 or rescued under section 16

(1) When the special police officer removing a girl under sub-section (4) of section 15 or rescuing a girl under sub-section (1) of section 16 fails to produce her immediately before the Magistrate as required by sub-section (5) of section 15 or sub-section (2) of section 16, he shall forthwith produce her before the nearest Magistrate of any class, who shall pass such orders as he deems proper for her safe custody until she is produced before the appropriate Magistrate.

(2) When the girl is produced before the appropriate Magistrate he shall after giving the girl an opportunity of being heard, cause an enquiry to be made as to the correctness of the information received under sub-section (1) of section 16 and the age of the girl and if satisfied that the information received is correct and the girl is under the age of twenty-one years he may, subject to the provisions of the next sub-section make an order that such girl be detained for such period as may be specified in the order in a protective home or such other custody as he, for reasons to be recorded in writing shall consider suitable :

Provided that such custody shall not be that of a person, or body of persons of a religious persuation different from that of the girl.

(3) In discharging his functions under sub-section (2) a Magistrate may summon a panel of five respectable persons, three of whom shall wherever practicable be women to assist him; and may for this purpose keep

a list of experienced social welfare workers, particularly women social welfare workers, in the field of suppression of immoral traffic in women and girls.

(4) Against every order under sub-section (2) an appeal shall be to the Sessions Judge whose decision on such appeal shall be final.

Closure of brothels and eviction of offenders from the premises

(1) A Magistrate may, on receipt of information from the police or otherwise that any house, room, place or any portion thereof within a distance of two hundred yards of any public place referred to in sub-section (1) of section 7, is being run or used as a brothel by any person, or is being used by prostitutes for carrying on their trade, issue notice on the owner, lessor or landlord of such house, room, place or portion or the agent of the owner, lessor or landlord or on the tenant, lessee, occupier of, or any other person in charge of such house, room, place or portion, to show cause within seven days of the receipt of the notice why the same should not be attached for improper use thereof; and if after hearing the person concerned the Magistrate is satisfied that the house, room, place or portion is being used as a brothel or for carrying on prostitution, then the Magistrate may pass orders-

(a) directing eviction of the occupier within seven days of the passing of the order from the house, room, place, or portion;

(b) directing that before letting it out during the period of one year immediately after passing the order the owner, lessor or landlord or the agent of the owner, lessor or landlord shall obtain the previous approval of the Magistrate;

provided that, if the Magistrate finds that the owner, lessor or landlord as well as the agent of the owner, lessor or landlord, was innocent of the improper use of the house, room, place or portion he may cause the same to be restored to the owner, lessor or landlord, or the agent of the owner, lessor or landlord, with a direction that the house, room, place or portion shall not be leased otherwise given possession of, to or for the benefit of the person who was allowing the improper use therein.

(2) A Court convicting a person of any offence under section 3 or section 7 may pass orders under sub-section (1), without further notice to such person to show cause as required in that sub-section.

(3) Orders passed by the Magistrate or court under sub-section (1) or sub-section (2) shall not be subject to appeal and shall not be stayed or set aside by the order of any Court, civil or criminal, and the said orders shall cease to have validity after the expiry of one year;

provided that where a conviction under section 3 or section 7 is set aside on appeal on the ground that such house, room, place or any portion thereof is not being run or used as a brothel or is not being used by prostitutes for carrying on their trade, any order passed by the trial Court under sub-section (1) shall also be set aside.

(4) Notwithstanding anything contained in any other law for the time being in force, when a Magistrate passes an order under sub-section (1), or a Court passes an order under sub-section (2), any lease or agreement under which the house, room, place or portion is occupied at the time shall become void and inoperative.

(5) When an owner, lessor or landlord, or the agent of such owner, lessor or landlord fails to comply with a direction given under clause (b) of sub-section (1) he shall be punishable with fine which may extend to five hundred rupees or when he fails to comply with a direction under the provision to that sub-section, he shall be deemed to have committed an offence under clause (b) of sub-section (2) of section 3 or clause (c) of sub-section (2) of section 7, as the case may be and punished accordingly.

Application for being kept in a protective home

(1) A woman or girl who is carrying on or is being made to carry on prostitution, may make an application to

the Magistrate within the local of whose jurisdiction she is carrying on, is being made to carry on, prostitution, for an order that she may be kept in a protective home.

(2) If after hearing the applicant and making such inquiry as he may consider necessary, the Magistrate is satisfied that an order should be made under this section then, he shall make an order, for reasons to be recorded, that the applicant be kept in a protective home for such period as may be specified in the order.

Removal of prostitute from any place

(1) A Magistrate on receiving information that any woman or girl residing in or frequenting any place within the local limits of his jurisdiction is a prostitute, may record, the substance of the information received and issue a notice to such woman or girl requiring her to appear before the Magistrate and show cause why she should not be required to remove herself from the place and be prohibited from re-entering it.

(2) Every notice issued under sub-section (1) shall be accompanied by a copy of a record aforesaid, and the copy shall be served along with the notice on the women or girl against whom the notice is issued.

(3) The Magistrate shall, after the service of the notice referred to in sub-section (2) proceed to inquire into the truth of the information received and after giving the women or girl an opportunity of adducing evidence, take such further evidence as he thinks fit, and if upon such inquiry it appears to him that such woman or girl is a prostitute, and that it is necessary in the interest of the general public that such woman or girl should be required to remove herself therefrom and be prohibited from re-entering the same, the Magistrate shall, by order in writing communicated to the woman or girl in the manner specified therein, require hereafter a date (to be specified in the order) which shall not be less than seven days from the date of the order, to remove herself from the place to such place whether

within or without the local limits of his jurisdiction, by such route or routes and within such time as may be specified in the order and also prohibit her from re-entering the place without the permission on writing of the Magistrate having jurisdiction over such place.

(4) Whoever-

(a) fails to comply with an order issued under this section, within the period specified therein or whilst an order prohibiting her from re-entering a place without permission is in force, re-enters the place without such permission, or

(b) knowing that any woman or girl has under this section been required to remove herself from the place and has not obtained the requisite permission to re-enter it, harbours or conceals such women or girl in the place shall be punishable with fine which may extend to two thousand rupees and in the case of a continuing offence with an additional fine which may extend to twenty rupees for every day after the first during which she or he has persisted in the offence.

Protective homes

(1) The State Government may in its discretion establish as many protective homes under this act as it thinks fit and such home when established shall be maintained in such manner as may be prescribed.

(2) No person or no authority other than State Government shall, after the commencement of this Act, establish or maintain any protective home except under and in accordance with the conditions of a licence issued under this section by the State Government.

(3) The State Government may, on application made to it in this behalf by a person or authority, issue to such person or authority a licence in the prescribed form for establishing and maintaining or as the case may be for maintaining a protective home and a licence so issued may contain such conditions as the State

Government may think fit to impose in accordance with the rules made under this Act :

provided that any such condition may require that the management of the protective home shall, wherever practicable, be entrusted to women :

provided further that a person or authority maintaining any protective home at the commencement of this Act shall be allowed a period of six months from such commencement to make an application for such licence.

(4) Before issuing a licence the State Government may require such officer or authority as it may appoint for this purpose, to make a full and complete investigation in respect to the application received in this behalf and report to it result of such investigation and in making any such investigation the officer or authority shall follow such procedure as may be prescribed.

(5) A licence unless sooner revoked, shall remain in force for such period as may be specified in the licence on applicable made in this behalf at least thirty days before the date of its expiration, be renewed for a like period.

(6) No licence issued or renewed under this Act shall be transferable.

(7) Where any person or authority to whom a licence has been granted under this Act or any servant of such person or authority commits a breach of any of the conditions thereof or any of the provisions of this Act or of any of the rules made under this Act, or where the State Government is not satisfied with the condition, management or superintendence of any protective home, the State Government may without prejudice to any other penalty which may have been incurred under this Act, for reasons to be recorded, revoke the licence by order in writing,

provided that no such order shall be made until an opportunity is given to the holder of the licence to show cause why the licence shall not be revoked.

(8) Where a licence in respect of a protective home has been revoked under the foregoing sub-section such

protective home shall cease to function from the date of such revocation.

(9) Subject to any rules that may be made in this behalf, the State Government may also vary or amend any licence issued or renewed under this Act.

(10) Whoever establishes or maintains a protective home except in accordance with the provisions of this section, shall be punishable in the case of a first offence with fine which may extend to one thousand rupees and in the case of second or subsequent offence with imprisonment for a term which may extend to one year, or with fine which may extend to two thousand rupees, or rupees, or with both.

Trials

No Court, inferior to that of a Magistrate as defined in clause (c) of section 2 shall try any offence under section 3, section 4, section 5, section 6, section 7 or section 8.

Power to make rules

(1) The State Government may, by notification in the Official Gazette, make rules for carrying out the purposes of this act.

(2) In particular and without prejudice to the generality of the foregoing powers, such rules may provide for-

(a) the notification of any place as a public place;

(b) the placing in custody of women and girls released under sub-section (1) of section 10 or for whose safe custody orders have been passed under sub-section (1) of section 17 and their maintenance;

(c) the detention and keeping in protective homes of women and girls under sub-section (2) of section 10, sub-section (2) of section 17 and section 19 and their maintenance;

(d) the carrying out of the provisions of section 11 regarding notification of residence or change of or absence from residence by released convicts;

(e) the delegation of authority to appoint the special police officer under sub-section (1) of section 13;

(f) the carrying into effect of the provisions of section 18;

(g) (i) the establishment, maintenance, management and superintendence of protective homes and the appointment, powers and duties of persons employed in such homes;

(ii) the form in which an application for a licence may be made and the particulars to be contained in such application;

(iii) the procedure for the issue or renewal of a licence, the time within which such licence shall be issued or renewed and the procedure to be followed in making a full and complete investigation in respect of an application for a licence;

(iv) the form of a licence and the conditions to be specified therein;

(v) the manner in which the accounts of a protective home shall be maintained and audited;

(vi) the maintenance of registers and statements by a licensee and the form of such registers and statements;

(vii) the care, treatment, maintenance, training, instruction, control and discipline of the inmates of protective homes;

(viii) the visits to and communication with such inmates;

(ix) the temporary detention of women and girls sentenced to detention in protective homes until arrangements are made for sending them to such homes;

(x) the transfer of a woman or girl from one protective home to another;

(xi) the transfer in pursuance of an order of the court from a protective home to a prison of a woman or girl found to be incorrigible or exercising bad influence upon other inmates of the protective home and the period of her detention in such prison;

(xii) the transfer to a protective home of women or girls sentenced under section 7 or section 8 and the period of their detention in such home;

(xiii) the discharge of inmates from a protective home either absolutely or subject to conditions, and their arrest in the event of breach of such conditions;

(xiv) the grant of permission to inmates to absent themselves for short periods;

(xv) the inspection of protective homes and other institutions in which women and girls may be kept, detained and maintained;

(h) any other matter which has to be, or may be, prescribed;

(3) In making any rule under clause (d) or clause (g) or sub-section (2) the State Government may provide that a breach thereof shall be punishable with fine which may extend to two hundred and fifty rupees.

(4) All rules made under this Act shall, as soon as may be after they are made, be laid before the State Legislature.

Act not be in derogation of certain other Acts

Nothing in this Act shall be construed to be in derogation of the provisions of the Reformatory Schools Act 1897 or any State Act enacted in modification of the said Act otherwise, relating to juvenile offenders.

Repeal and Savings

(1) As from the date of the coming into force in any State of the provisions other than section 1 of this Act, all State Acts relating to suppression of immoral traffic in women and girls or to the prevention of prostitution,

in force in that State immediately before such date shall stand repealed.

(2) Notwithstanding the repeal by this Act of any state Act referred to in sub-section (1) anything done or any action taken (including any direction given, any register, rule or order made, any restriction imposed) under the provisions of such State Act shall in so far as such thing is not inconsistent with the provisions of this Act be deemed to have been done or taken under the provisions of this Act as if the said provisions were in force when such thing was done or such action was taken and shall continue in force accordingly until superseded by any thing done or any action taken under this Act.

Explanation: In this section the expression 'State Act' includes a 'Provincial Act'.

(F-1) The Suppression of Immoral Traffic in Women and Girls (Amendment) Act, 1986

(Act No. 44 of 1986) [8th September, 1986]

An Act further to amend the Suppression of Immoral Traffic in Women and Girls Act, 1956.

Be it enacted by Parliament in the Thirty-seventh Year of the Republic of India as follows:

Short Title and Commencement

(1) This Act may be called the Suppression of Immoral Traffic in Women and Girls (Amendment) Act, 1986.

(2) It shall come into force on such date as the Central Government may, by notification in the official Gazette, appoint.

Amendment of long title

In the Suppression of Immoral Traffic in Women and Girls Act, 1956 (hereinafter referred to as the principal Act), in the long title, for the words "the suppression of immoral traffic in women and girls", the words "the prevention of immoral traffic" shall be substituted.

Amendment of Section 1

In S.1. of the principal Act, in sub-sec.(1), for the words "the suppression of immoral traffic in women and girls", the words and brackets "the immoral traffic (Prevention)" shall be substituted.

Substitution of references to certain expressions by certain other expressions

Throughout the principal Act [except sub-sec.(3) and (4) of S.6], unless otherwise expressly provided, for the words "women and girls" and "woman or girl", wherever they occur, the words "persons" and "person" shall respectively be substituted, and such other consequential amendments as the rules of grammar may require shall also be made.

Amendment of Section 2

In S. 2 of the principal Act, (a) in Cl. (a), for the words "of prostitution" the words "of sexual exploitation or abuse" shall be substituted;

(b) after Cl. (a), the following clause shall be inserted, namely:

'(aa) "child" means a person who has not completed the age of sixteen years;'

(c) existing Cl. (aa) shall be re-lettered as Cl. (b) thereof, and in Cl. (b) as so re-lettered, for the words "female undertrials", the word "undertrials" shall be substituted:

(d) existing Cl. (b) shall be omitted;

(e) after Cl. (c) the following clauses shall be inserted, namely:

'(ca) "major" means a person who has completed the age of eighteen years;

(cb) "minor" means a person who has completed the age of sixteen years but has not completed the age of sixteen years;';

(f) for Cl. (f), the following clause shall be substituted. namely :

'(f) "prostitution" means the sexual exploitation or abuse of persons for commerical purposes, and the expression "prostitute" shall be construed accordingly;'

(g) in Cl. (g),-

(i) in the opening portion, after the words "kept under this Act", the words "and where appropriate technically qualified persons, equipment and other facilities have been provided" shall be inserted;

(ii) in sub-cl. (i), for the words "female undertrials", the word "undertrials" shall be substituted;

(h) for Cl. (j), the following clause shall be substituted, namely:

'(j) "trafficking police officer" means a police officer appointed by the Central Government under sub-sec. (4) of S. 13'.

Amendment of Section 3

In S. 3 of the principal Act, after sub-sec. (2), the following sub-section shall be inserted, namely:

"(2A) for the purposes of sub-sec. (2), it shall be presumed, until the contrary is proved that any person referred to in Cl. (a) or Cl (b) of that sub-section, is knowingly allowing the premises or any part thereof to be used as a brothel or, as the case may be, has knowledge that the premises or anypart thereof are being used as a brothel, if—

(a) a report is published in newspaper having circulation in the area in which such person resides to the effect that the premises or any part thereof have been found to be used for prostitution as a result of a search made under this Act; or

(b) a copy of the list of all things found during the search referred to in Cl. (a) is given to such person."

Amendment of Section 4

In S.4 of the principal Act, in sub-sec. (1), -

(a) for the words "a woman or girl", the words "any other person" shall be substituted;

(b) after the words "or with both", the words "and where such earnings relate to the prostitution of a child or a minor, shall be punishable with imprisonment for a term of not less than seven years" shall be inserted.

Amendment of Section 5

In section 5 of the principal Act -

(a) in sub-section (1), for the portion beginning with the words "shall be punishable" and ending with the words "two thousand rupees", the following shall be substituted, namely:

"shall be punishable on conviction with rigorous imprisonment for a term of not less than three years and not more than seven years and also with fine which may extend to two thousand rupees, and if any offence under this sub-section is committed against the will of any person, the punishment of imprisonment for a term of seven years shall extend to imprisonment for a term of fourteen years:

provided that if the person in respect of whom an offence committed under this sub-section-

(i) is a child, the punishment provided under this sub-section shall extend to rigorous imprisonment for a term of not less than seven years but may extend to life; and

(ii) is a minor, the punishment provided under this sub-section shall extend to rigorous imprisonment for a term of not less than seven years and not more than fourteen years."

(b) sub-section (2) shall be omitted.

Amendment of Section 6

In section 6 of the principal Act,

(a) in sub-sec. (1)-

(i) In the opening portion, for the words "any woman or girl, whether with or without her consent", the words "any other person, whether with or without his consent" shall be substituted

(ii) in Cl. (b), for the words "that she may have sexual intercourse with any man other than her lawful husband", the words "that such person may have sexual intercourse with a person who is not the spouse of such person" shall be substituted;

(iii) for the portion beginning with the words "on first conviction" and ending with the words "two thousand rupees", the following shall be substituted, namely:

"on conviction, with imprisonment of either description for a term which shall not be less than seven years but which may be for life or for a term which may extend to ten years and shall also be liable to fine.

Provided that the Court may, for adequate and special reasons to be mentioned in the judgement, impose a sentence of imprisonment for a term of less than seven years",

(b) for sub-sec. (2), the following sub-sections shall be substituted, namely—

(2) Where any person is found with a child in a brothel, it shall be presumed, unless the contrary is proved, that he has committed an offence under sub-sec. (1),

(2A) where a child or minor found in a brothel, is, on medical examination, detected to have been sexually abused, it shall be presumed, unless the contrary is proved, that the child or minor has been detained for purposes of prostitution or, as the case may be, has been sexually exploited for commercial purposes."

Amendment of Section 7

In section 7 of the principal Act—

(a) after sub-sec. (1), the following sub section shall be inserted, namely—

(1A) Where an offence committed under sub-sec. (1) is in respect of a child or minor, the person committing the offence shall be punishable with imprisonment of either description for a term which shall not be less than seven years but which may be for life or for a term which may extend to ten years and shall also be liable to fine.

Provided that the Court may, for adequate and special reasons to be mentioned in the judgement, impose a sentence of imprisonment for a term of less than seven years."

(b) in sub-sec. (2) for the words " which may extend to two hundred rupees", the following shall be substituted, namely;

"which may extend to two hundred rupees, and if the public place or premises happen to be a hotel, the licence for carrying on the business of such hotel under any law for the time being in force shall also liable to be suspended for a period of not less than three months but which may extend to one year;

provided that if an offence committed under this sub-section is in respect of a child or minor in a hotel, such licence shall also be liable to be cancelled."

Explanation: For the purposes of this sub-section, "hotel" shall have the meaning as in Cl. (6) of S. 2 of the Hotel-Receipts Tax Act, 1980.

Amendment of Section 8

To section 8 of the principal Act, the following provision shall be added, namely:

"provided that where an offence under this section is committed by a man, he shall be punishable with imprisonment for a period of not less that seven days but which may extend to three months."

Amendment of Section 9

In section 9 of the principal Act.,

(a) in sub-sec. (1),-

(i) the brackets and figure "(1)" shall be omitted;

(ii) for the portion beginning with the words "shall be punishable" and ending with the words "one thousand rupees", the following shall be substituted, namely:

"shall be punishable on conviction with imprisonment of either description for a term which shall not be less than seven years but which may be for life or for a term which may extend to ten years and shall also be liable to fine;

provided that the Court may, for adequate and special reasons to be mentioned in the judgement, impose a sentence of imprisonment for a term of less than seven years".

(b) sub-sec. (2) shall be omitted.

Omission of Sections 10 and 12

Sections 10 and 12 of the principal Act shall be omitted.

Amendment of Section 10A

In sub-sec. (1), of S. 10A of the principal Act, in Cl. (a), the words, brackets and figures "and is not released under sub-sec. (1) or sub-sec. (2) of S. 10" shall be omitted.

Amendment of Section 13

In section 13 of the principal Act, after sub-sec. (3), the following sub-section shall be inserted, namely:

"(4) The Central Government may, for the purpose of investigating any offence under this Act or under any other law for the time being in force dealing with sexual exploitation of persons and committed in more than one State, appoint such number of police officers as trafficking police officers and they shall exercise all the powers and discharge all the functions as are exercisable by special police officers under this Act with the modification that they shall exercise such powers and discharge such functions in relation to the whole of India."

Amendment of Section 15

In section 15 of the principal Act,-

(a) after the words "special police officer", wherever they

occur, the words "or the trafficking police officer, as the case may be," shall be inserted;

(b) for sub-sec. (4) the following sub-section shall be substituted, namely:

"(4) The special police officer of the trafficking police officer, as the case may be entering any premises under sub-sec. (1) shall be entitled to remove therefrom all the persons found therein".

(c) after sub-sec. (5), the following sub-section shall be inserted, namely:

'(5A) any person who is produced before a magistrate under sub-sec. (5), shall be examined by a registered medical practitioner for the purposes of determination of the age of such person, or for the detection of any injuries as a result of sexual abuse or for the presence of any sexually transmitted diseases."

Explanation: In this sub-section, "registered medical practiotioner" has the same meaning as in the Indian Medical Council Act., 1956;

(d) after sub-sec. (6), the following subsection shall be inserted, namely:

'(6A) The special police officer or the trafficking police officer, as the case may be making a search under this section shall be accompanied by at least two women police officers, and where any woman or girl removed under sub-sec. (4) is required to be interrogated, it shall be done by a woman police officer and if no woman police officer is available, the interrogation shall be done only in the presence of a lady member of a recognised welfare institution or organisation.

Explanation: For the purposes of this sub-section and S. 17 A, "recognised welfare institution or organisation" means such institution or organisation as may be recognised in this behalf by the State Government.

Amendment of Section 16

In sub-sec. (1) of S. 16 of the principal Act, for Cls. (a) and (b), the words " any person is living or is carrying on, or is being made to carry on, prostitution in a brothel," shall be substituted.

Amendment of Section 17

In sub-Sec. (3) of S. 17 of the principal Act, for the words "provided that ", the following shall be substituted, namely:

"provided that where a person rescued under S. 16 is a child or minor, it shall be open to the magistrate to place such child or minor in any institution established or recognised under any Children Act for the time being in force in any State for the safe custody of children;

provided further that".

Insertion of new Section 17A

After section 17 of the principal Act, the following section shall be inserted, namely:

"17A. Conditions to be observed before placing persons rescued under Section 16 to parents or guardians

Notwithstanding anything contained in sub-sec. (2) of S. 17, the magistrate making an inquiry under S. 17 may, before passing an order for handing over any person rescued under S. 16 to the parents, guardian or husband, satisfy himself about the capacity or genuineness of the parents, guardian or husband to keep such persons by causing any investigation to be made by a recognised welfare institution or organisation.".

Amendment of Section 18

In S. 18 of the principal Act-

(a) in sub-sec. (1) in Cl. (b), after the words "period of one year", the words and figures "or in a case where a child or minor has been found in such house, room, place or portion during a search under S. 15, during the period of three years," shall be inserted;

(b) in sub-sec. (3), for the words "expiry of one year", the words "expiry of one year or three years, as the case may be" shall be substituted.

Insertion of new Section 21A

After S. 21 of the principal Act, the following section shall be inserted, namely:

"**21A. Production of records** : Every person or authority who is licensed under sub-sec. (3) of S. 21 to establish or maintain or, as the case may be, for maintaining, a protective home or corrective institution shall whenever required by a court, produce the records and other documents maintained by such home or institution before such Court.".

Insertion of new Section 22AA

After S. 22A of the principal Act, the following shall be inserted, namely:

"22AA-Power of Central Government to establish special Courts

(1) If the Central Government is satisfied that it is necessary for the purpose of providing for speedy trial of offences under this Act and committed in more than one State, it may by notification in the Official Gazette and after consultation with the High Court concerned, establish one or more Courts of Judicial Magistrates of the first class or Metropolitan Magistrates for the trial of such offences.

(2) The provisions of S. 22A shall so far as may be apply to the Courts established under sub-sec. (1), as they apply to Courts established under that section."

Amendment of Section 23

In sub-sec. (2) of S. 23 of the principal Act, for Cl. (b), the following clause shall be substituted, namely :

"(b) the placing in custody of persons for whose safe custody orders have been passed under sub-sec. (1) of S. 17 and their maintenance."

Amendment of the Schedule

In the schedule to the principal Act, the figures, brackets and words "12(4) Metropolitan Magistrate or Judicial Magistrate of the first class" shall be omitted.

(G) Indian Penal Code: Sections 312 to 316

Section 312: Causing miscarriage

Whoever voluntarily causes a woman with a child to miscarry, shall, if such miscarriage be not caused in good faith for the purpose of saving the life of the woman, be punished with imprisonment of either description for a term which may extend to three years, or with fine, or with both; and, if the woman be quick with child, shall be punished with imprisonment of either description for a term which may extend to seven years, and shall also be liable to fine.

Explanation: A woman who causes herself to miscarry, is within the meaning of this section.

Section 313: Causing miscarriage without woman's consent

Whoever, commits the offence defined in the last preceding section without the consent of the woman, whether the woman is quick with child or not, shall be punished with imprisonment for life, or with imprisonment of either description for a term which may extend to ten years and shall be liable to fine.

Section 314: Death caused by act done with intent to cause miscarriage

Whoever, with intent to cause the miscarriage of a woman with child, does any act which caused the death of such woman, shall be punished with imprisonment of either description for a term which may extend to ten years, and shall also be liable to fine.

If act is done without woman's consent - and if the act is done without the consent of the woman, shall be punished either with imprisonment for life, or with punishment above mentioned.

Explanation: It is not essential to this offence that the offender should know that the act is likely to cause death.

Section 315: Act done with intent to prevent child being born alive or to cause it to die after birth

Whoever, before the birth of any child does any act with the intention thereby preventing that child from being born alive or causing it to die after its birth, shall, if such act not caused in good faith for the purpose of saving the life of the mother be punished with imprisonment of either description for a term which may extend to ten years, or with fine, or with both.

Section 316: Causing death of quick unborn child by act amounting to culpable homicide

Whoever, does any act under such circumstances, that if thereby causes death he would be guilty of culpable homicide, and does by such act cause the death of a quick unborn child, shall be punished with imprisonment of either description for a term which may extend to ten years, and shall also be liable to fine.

(H) The Medical Termination of Pregnancy Act, 1971

An Act to provide for the termination of certain pregnancies by registered medical practitioners and for matters connected therewith or incidental thereto.

Be it enacted by Parliament in Twenty-second Year of the Republic of India as follows:

Short title, extent and commencement

(1) This Act may be called the Medical termination of Pregnancy Act, 1971.

(2) It extends to the whole of India except the State of Jammu and Kashmir.

(3) It shall come into force on such date as the Central Government may, by notification in the Official Gazette, appoint.

Definitions

In this Act, unless the context otherwise requires-

(a) "guardian" means a person having the care of the person of a minor or lunatic;

(b) "lunatic" has the meaning assigned to it in Section 3 of the Indian Lunancy Act, 1912 (4 of 1912);

(c) "minor" means a person who, under the provisions of the Indian Majority Act, 1875 (9 of 1875) is to be deemed not to have attained his majority;

(d) "registered medical practitioner" means a medical practitioner who possess any recognised medical qualification as defined to CL. (h) of Section 2 of the Indian Medical Council Act, 1956 (102 of 1956), whose name has been entered in a State Medical Register and who has such experience of training in gynaecology and obstetrics as may be prescribed by rules made under this Act.

When pregnancies may be terminated by registered medical practitioners-

(1) Notwithstanding anything contained in the Indian Penal Code (45 of 1860), a registered medical practitioner shall not be guilty of any offence under that code or under any other law for the time being in force, if any pregnancy is terminated by him in accordance with the provisions of this Act.

(2) Subject to the provisions of sub-section 4, a pregnancy may be terminated by registered medical practitioner-

(a) where the length of the pergnancy does not exceed twelve weeks, if such medical practitioner is, or

(b) where the length of the pregnancy exceeds twelve

weeks but does not exceed twenty weeks, if not less than two registered medical practitioners are, of the opinion formed in good faith, that-

(i) the continuance of the pregnancy would involve a risk to the life of the pregnant woman or of grave injury to her physical or mental health; or

(ii) there is a substantial risk that if the child were born, it would suffer from such physical or mental abnormalities as to be seriously handicapped.

Explanation I: Where pregnancy is alleged by the pregnant woman to have been caused by rape, the anguish caused by such pregnancy shall be presumed to constitute a grave injury to the mental health of the pregnant woman.

Explanation II: Where any pregnancy occurs as a result of failure of any device or method used by any married woman or her husband for the purpose of limiting the number of children, the anguish caused by such unwanted pregnancy may be presumed to constitute a grave injury to the mental health of the pregnant woman.

(3) In determining whether the continuance of a pregnancy would involve such risk of injury to the health as is mentioned in sub-section (2), account may be taken of the pregnant woman's actual or reasonably foreseeable environment.

(4) (a) No pregnancy of a woman, who has not attained the age of eighteen years, or who having attained the age of eighteen years, is a lunatic, shall be terminated except with the consent in writing of her guardian.

(b) Save as otherwise provided in clause (a) no pregnancy shall be terminated except with the consent of the pregnant woman.

Place where pregnancy may be terminated

No termination of pregnancy shall be made in accordance with this Act at any place other than-

(a) a hospital established or maintained by Government, or

(b) a place for the time being approved for the purpose of this Act by Government.

Section 3 and 4 when not to apply

(1) The Provisions of Section 4, and so much of the provisions of sub-section (2) of Section 3 as relate to the length of the pregnancy and the opinion of not less than two registered medical practitioners, shall not apply to the termination of a pregnancy by a registered medical practitioner in a case where he is of opinion, formed in good faith, that the termination of such pregnancy is immediately necessary to save the life of the pregnant woman.

(2) Notwithstanding anything contained in the Indian Penal Code, the termination of a pregnancy by a person who is not a registered medical practitioner shall be an offence punishable under that Code, and that Code shall, to this extent stand modified.

Explanation: For the purposes of this Section, so much of the provisions of Clause (d) of Section 2 as relate to the possession, by a registered medical practitioner, of experience or training in gynaecology and obstetrics shall not apply.

Power to make rules

(1) The Government may, by notification in the Official Gazette, make rules to carry out the provisions of this Act.

(2) In particular, and without prejudice to the generality of the foregoing power, such rules may provide for all or any of the following matters, namely:

(a) the experience or training, or both, which a registered medical practitioner shall have if he intends to terminate any pregnancy under this Act, and

(b) such other matters as are required to be, or may be, provided by rules made under this Act.

(3) Every rule made by the Central Government under this

Act shall be laid, as soon as may be after it is made, before each House of Parliament while it is in session for a total period of thirty days which may be comprised in one session or in two successive sessions, and if, before the expiry of the session in which it is so laid or the session immediately following, both Houses agree in making any modification in the rule or both thereafter have effect, as the case may be, so, however that any such modification or annulment shall be without prejudice to the validity of anything previously done under that rule.

Power to make regulations

(1) The State Government may, by regulations,

(a) require any such opinion as is referred to in sub-section 2 of Section 3 to be certified by a registered medical practitioner or practitioners concerned, in such form and at such time as may be specified in such regulations, and the preservation or disposal of such certificates.

(b) require any registered medical practitioner who terminates pregnancy to give intimation of such termination and such other information relating to the termination as may be specified in such regulations;

(2) The intimation given and the information furnished in pursuance of regulations made by virtue of clause (b) of sub-section (1) shall be given or furnished as the case may be, to the Chief Medical Officer of the State.

(3) Any person who wilfully contravenes or wilfully fails to comply with the requirements of any regulation made under sub-section 1 shall be liable to be punished with fine which may extend to one thousand rupees.

Protection of action taken in good faith

No suit or other legal proceeding shall be against any registered medical practitioner for any damage caused or likely to be caused by anything which is in good faith done or intended to be done under this Act.

Bibliography

(1) Aggarwal, Partap Chand, *Halfway to Equality*, Manohar Publications, Delhi, 1983.

(2) Anderson, Norman, *Liberty, Law and Justice*, Stevans and Sons Ltd., London, 1978.

(3) Arputhamurthy, Savitri; *Women Work and Discrimination*, APH Publishing Corporation, New Delhi.

(4) Austin, Granville, *The Indian Constitution: Cornerstone of a Nation*, Oxford University Press, Bombay, 1979.

(5) Basu, Durga Das, *Human Rights in Constitutional Law*, Prentice Hall of India, New Delhi, 1994.

(6) Batra, Manjula, *Protection of Human Rights in Criminal Justice Administration: A Study of the Rights of Accused in India and Soviet Union*, Deep & Deep Publications, New Delhi, 1987.

(7) Batra, T.S., *Human Rights: A Critique*, Metropolitan, New Delhi, 1979.

(8) Bhattarcharjee, A.M., *Hindu Law and Constitution*, Eastern Law House, New Delhi, 1994.

(9) Browne, J.C., *Indian Infanticide: Its Origins, Progress and Suppression*, London, 1857.

(10) Brownlie, Lan, (ed); *Basic Documents On Human Rights*, Clarendon Press, Oxford, 1971.

(11) Buergenthal, Thomas; *Human Rights, International Law & The Helsinki Accord*, Allied Publications, New Delhi, 1979.

(12) Chitkara, M.G., *Human Rights: Commitment and Betrayal*, APH Publishing Corporation, New Delhi.

(13) Crossette, Barbara, *India: Facing the Twenty-First Century*, Indiana University Press, Bloomington, 1993.

(14) Dacs, Erica-Irene A., *Freedom of the Individual under Law*, United Nations, New York, 1998.

(15) Devasia, Leelamma and V.V. Devasia, *Girl Child in India*, APH Publishing Corporation, New Delhi

(16) --, *Empowering Women for the Sustainable Development*, APH Publishing Corporation, New Delhi.

(17) Diwan, Paras, *Modern Hindu Law: Codified and Uncodified*, Allahabad Law Agency, Allahabad, 1990.

(18) Diwan Paras, *Dowry and Protection to Married Women*, Deep & Deep Publications, New Delhi, 1995.

(19) Donnelly, Jack, *Universal Human Rights in Theory and Practice*, Cornell University Press, Ithaea, 1989.

(20) Fyzee, Asaf A. A., *Outlines of Mohammadan Law*, Oxford Univeristy Press, Delhi, 1993,.

(21) Ghosh, S. K., *The World of Prostitute*, APH Publishing Coporation, New Delhi.

(22) - - *Women and Crime;* APH Publishing Corporation, New Delhi.

(23) - -, *Torture and Rape in Police Custody*, APH Publishing Corporation, New Delhi.

(24) - -, *Environment and Women Development : Lessons from the Third World*, APH Publishng Corporation, New Delhi.

(25) Gillies, David, *Between Principle and Practice: Human Rights in North-South Relations*, McGill-Queen's University Press, 1998.

(26) Hansaria, B. L., *Right to Life and Liberty under the Constitution*, N. M. Tripathi, Bombay, 1993.

(27) Hasan, Shariful, *Supreme Court: Fundamental Rights and Directive Principles*, Deep Publications, New Delhi, 1981.

(28) Iyer, V. R. Krishna, *Indian Social Justice in Crisis*, Affiliated North-East Press, New Delhi, 1983.

(29) - -, *Human Rights and the Law*, Vedpal Law House, Indore, 1986.

(30) Jaswal, Paramjit S., *Directive Principles, Jurisprudence and Socio-Economic Justice in India*, Ashish Publishing House, New Delhi, 1995.

(31) - -, and Nishatha Jaswal, *Human Rights and the Law*, APH Publishing Corporation, New Delhi, 1996.

(32) Kalaiah, A.B., *Human Rights in International Law*, Deep and Deep Publications, New Delhi, 1986.

(33) Kant, Anjani, *Women and the Law*, APH Publishing Corporation, New Delhi, 1997.

(34) Ketan, Sanjay, *Working Women and Modernization*, APH Publishing Corporation, New Delhi, 1997.

(35) Khanna, M.R, *Judiciary in India and Judicial Process*, Ajay Law House, Calcutta, 1985.

(36) Kitchlu, T.N, *Widows in India*, APH Publishing Corporation, New Delhi.

(37) Kuppuswamy, B., *Social Change in India*, Vikas Publication, Bombay, 1972.

(38) Mahanta, Jodeshwari, *Sex, Crime and Society*, APH Publishing Corporation, New Delhi, 1997.

(39) Mallick, Ross, *Development Ethnicity and Human Rights in India*, Sage Publications, New Delhi, 1998.

(40) Pandey, J.N., *Constitutional Law of India*, Central Law Agency, Allahabad, 1993

(41) Pant, Niranjan, *Status of Girl Child and Women in India*, APH Publishing Corporation, New Delhi, 1995.

(42) Qureshi, M.A, *Muslim Law of Marriage, Divorce and Maintenance*, Deep and Deep Publications, New Delhi.

(43) Rao, N. J. Usha, *Women in a Developing Society*, APH Publishing Corporation, New Delhi.

(44) Sehgal, B.P.S, *Women, Birth and the Law*, Deep & Deep Publications, New Delhi.

(45) Shams, Shamshuddin, *Women, Law and Social Change*, APH Publishing Corporation, New Delhi.

(46) Sharma, O.C, *Crime Against Women*, APH Publishing Corporation, New Delhi.

(47) Sharma, Vijay, *Protection to Women in Matrimonial Home*, Deep & Deep Publications, New Delhi.

(48) Singh, Nagendra Kumar, *Divine Prostitution*, APH Publishing Corporation, New Delhi.

(49) Singh, S.S., *Unification of Divorce Laws in India*, Deep & Deep Publications, New Delhi.

(50) Sinha, Anjana Maitra, *Women in Changing Society*, APH Publishing Corporation, New Delhi.

(51) Swarup, Hari, *For Whome the Law is Made?*, Veena Publications, New Delhi, 1981.

(52) Swarup, Jagdish, *Human Rights and Fundmental Freedoms*, N.M. Tripathi, Bombay, 1975.

(53) United Nations, *The United Nations and Human Rights*, United Nations, New York; 1984.

(54) United Nations, *Human Rights: Questions and Answers*, United Nations, New York, 1987.

(55) Upadhyaya, Neelam and Rekha Panday, *Women in India: Past and Present*, First Published, 1990.

(56) Vadackumchery, James, *Human Rights and the Police in India*, APH Publishing Corporation, New Delhi.

Articles

(1) *Anklesaria, Shahnaz*, "Women and the Law: Some Basic Questions"; *The Statesman*, New Delhi, 28 February, 1985

(2) - -, "Law Purposes, non Disposes", *The Statesman*, New Delhi, 14 August, 1984.

(3) - -, "Gender Bias Within Indian Legislation", *The Statesman*, New Delhi, 19 April, 1985.

(4) - -, "Gender Bias in Succession Law", *The Statesman,* New Delhi, 26 March, 1985.

(5) - -, "Male Chauvinism is Ingrained in Us, "*The Statemam,* New Delhi, 18 June, 1985.

(6) - -, "Laws which Discriminate Against Women", *The Statesman,* New Delhi, 21 June 1984.

(7) Anthony O'Amato, "The Concept of Human Rights in International Law", *Columbia Law Review,* 82, 1982.

(8) Ateeq, Nasir; "Dowry Laws" *The Pioneer,* Lucknow, 9 April, 1996.

(9) Chowdhary, Neerza, "SITA Messed up by Hasty Amendment", *The Pioneer,* Lucknow, 21 February, 1992.

(10) Donnelly, Jack, "Human Rights and Development", *World Politics,* Vol. 36, No. 4, January 1984.

(11) Govil, Anju, "No to Equality if Means Alimony", *The Pioneer,* Lucknow, 15 February, 1992.

(12) Hingorani, R.C., "Human Rights in Developing Countries", *Indian Bar Review, X,* 1983.

(13) Kala, Arvind, "Need to Legalise Prostitution" *The Pioneer,* Lucknow, 30 March, 1996.

(14) Kapur, Naina, "No Gender Perspective even in (Progressive) Legislation, *The Pioneer,* Lucknow, 30 December, 1991.

(15) Kranti, Vijay, "Changul Se Mukt", *India Today (Hindi), 15* September, 1991.

(16) Noorani, A.G., Civil Liberties: Indias Report to U.N. on Human Rights", *Economic and Political Weekly,* xix, 1984.

(17) Sarkar, Lolita, "Constitutional Guarantees. The Unequal Sex," *Occasional Paper No 8,* Centre for Women's Development Studies, New Delhi, 1986.

(18) Tyagi, K. Yogesh, "Third World Response to Human Rights"; *Indian Journal of International Law,* 21, 1981.

Index